Murder Most Vile
Volume 27

18 Truly Shocking
Murder Cases

Robert Keller

**Please Leave Your Review of This Book at
http://bit.ly/kellerbooks**

ISBN: 9781695538962

© 2019 by Robert Keller

robertkellerauthor.com

Table of Contents

Collateral Damage

Thomas J. Capano had lived a gilded life. His father, Louis Capano, was a highly successful building contractor and real estate developer, and Thomas had grown up never wanting for anything. After graduating high school, he'd attended college and then law school, obtaining a law degree. Thereafter, he'd returned to his home state of Delaware where his unbroken run of success showed no sign of slowing down. He became a high-profile, well-connected lawyer, a state prosecutor, a partner in one of the state's most prominent law firms, counsel to Governor Michael N. Castle, a power broker in Delaware politics. He was also a control freak and a serial philanderer. Married and the father of four daughters, Capano nonetheless kept a string of mistresses on call. In 1996, one of them was Anne Marie Fahey, the appointments secretary to then-Governor Thomas R. Carper.

Anne Marie was an attractive woman, tall, elegant and blue-eyed, with a mop of curly brunette hair. Yet despite her looks and the successful career that she had carved out for herself, despite her outwardly vivacious nature, she was deeply insecure. That made her an easy mark for a predator like Thomas Capano. Within weeks of their first meeting in 1994, he had seduced her. Not long after that, she recorded in her diary that she was in love with him. It was a flame that would flicker only briefly before Anne Marie learned the true nature of the man she had fallen for. Capano was a jealous and extremely possessive individual. It was okay for him to flit from one mistress to another, but he expected absolute loyalty from her. He also expected her to be at his beck and call.

By September 1995, Anne Marie had grown tired of being Tom Capano's plaything. That was the month that she agreed to go on a blind date with a man named Michael Scanlon, at that time the community affairs chief of MBNA America Bank. Scanlon was handsome, he was charming, he was closer to her own age and, most importantly, he was single. Before long, Anne Marie had fallen for him and they started dating.

But Thomas Capano was not about to let Anne Marie walk out on him that easily. Their affair would be over when he said it was, not before. He continued to exert control over her, bending her to his will by preying on her insecurities, by alternately cajoling and threatening, by all but stalking her. Anne Marie endured this situation for months, until June 1996, when she finally summoned the courage to tell Capano that it was over. He accepted her decision with apparent good grace, asking only that she join him for one last dinner, at his favorite Italian restaurant, Ristorante Panorama in Philadelphia. The date was June 27, 1996, and the couple were seen together at the restaurant that night, leaving at around 9:30. Anne Marie Fahey was never seen alive again.

Anne Marie's disappearance was not noticed until two days later, when she failed to keep a dinner date with Michael Scanlon. Her family then went to her apartment on Washington Street in Wilmington. They found it orderly but empty. They also found her diary, in which she had made a note of her dinner date with Capano. In the same entry, she had described Capano as a "jealous maniac."

The following day, June 30, Wilmington Police officers arrived at Thomas Capano's house to question him regarding Anne Marie's disappearance. Capano seemed shocked at the news but was nonetheless cooperative, even allowing the officers to search his house and car without a warrant. He admitted to dining with Anne Marie on the night she went missing but insisted that he'd driven her straight home. He had gone up to her apartment for only a few minutes, he said, to have a look at her faulty air conditioner. He'd left at around ten and had not seen her since. Neither did he have any idea where she might be. The police had no reason to disbelieve his version of events.

But already, the case was causing a stir. There were rumors that Capano had been stalking Anne Marie, threatening her. Those rumors, apparently, reached much further than Wilmington. On July 5, President Bill Clinton called Delaware Governor Carper and offered the FBI's help in the search for Anne Marie. Meanwhile, Thomas Capano, annoyed at another police search of his home, was lawyering up, appointing former Delaware Attorney General Charles M. Oberly III to represent him.

That was probably a good thing because the FBI had been checking Capano's credit card records and had uncovered an interesting anomaly. On June 29, Capano had purchased a carpet. Nothing unusual in that except that Capano had by now separated from his wife and was living in rented accommodation. Why would he buy a carpet for a furnished apartment that he was only renting? The answer may have been in testimony obtained from the Capanos' maid. She testified that a carpet and love seat at the family home had recently been replaced.

And the circumstantial evidence against Capano kept stacking up. The Feds learned from an employee of the family construction business that he had been ordered by Capano's brother, Louis Jr., to haul away a half-filled dumpster on July 1. The dumpster had contained a carpet and a love seat. Another piece of the puzzle fell into place when it was discovered that Capano's youngest brother, Gerard, had sold his fishing boat at around the time, offering the buyer a discount as the boat was missing its anchor.

From all of these disparate snippets of information, the FBI was starting to put together a picture of what had happened to Anne Marie Fahey. They believed that Capano had driven her back to his home after dinner. There, he'd shot her, wrapped her in a carpet and driven her to his brother's fishing boat. Anne Marie's body was then transported to a spot off the coast where it was thrown overboard, weighed down by the boat's anchor. It seemed a likely theory. But could they prove it?

On July 31, investigators, led by Assistant U.S. Attorney Colm F. Connolly, carried out an 11-hour search of Capano's home and turned up their most valuable clue yet, two spots of blood which would later be forensically matched to Anne Marie Fahey. That was enough to haul Capano before a federal grand jury, but still he refused to admit to anything. It was only when the Feds turned their spotlight on the lesser players in the drama that they began to make progress in the case.

The first to crack was Gerard Capano, Tom's youngest brother and alibi witness. On November 8, he showed up with his attorney at the FBI offices and said that he had information to share. According to him, he had helped Thomas dump a body off Stone Harbor on June 28, 1996. Gerard said that the body had first been tossed into the ocean inside a large cooler box. However, the plastic container had stubbornly refused to sink, even when perforated by a couple of blasts from a shotgun. Tom Capano had then hauled the box back on board, removed the body and weighed it down with the ship's anchor. It had then been thrown back overboard, sinking almost immediately.

According to Gerard, he had not participated in the impromptu burial and could not even bring himself to look at the young woman's body. He did, however, admit that he had helped Thomas dispose of a blood-stained sofa in a dumpster at Louis Capano's construction site. Louis would confirm this two days later, when he showed up with his own attorney. He also confessed that he had ordered the removal of the dumpster with the bloodied sofa inside.

Thomas Capano's inner circle had now turned on him, implicating him in the death of Anne Marie Fahey. Despite the absence of a body or murder weapon, he was arrested on November 12 and charged with murder. The following day, the police received another boost to their case when a fisherman handed over a plastic cooler box, perforated by shotgun pellets. According to the man, he had found the box floating in the Atlantic in early July 1996.

On December 22, a New Castle County grand jury handed down a murder indictment against Thomas Capano, and on January 8, 1997, he answered that indictment with a not guilty plea. Meanwhile, the evidence continued to stack up against him. Prosecutors had been desperate to locate the murder weapon, and while they had been unsuccessful in doing so, they had the next best thing on February 4. That was the day that Deborah MacIntyre, another of Capano's mistresses, told police that she had bought a .22-caliber Beretta pistol for him on May 15, 1996 – six weeks before Anne Marie Fahey went missing. Investigators were prepared to venture that the weapon was currently at the bottom of the ocean, but this nonetheless was a vital piece of evidence, since it put the potential murder weapon in Capano's hands.

Thomas Capano went on trial for murder on October 6, 1997. He had assembled at team of four stellar attorneys to represent him, led by eminent Boston litigator, Joseph Oteri, and dubbed by the media as the "Dream Team." However, Capano would prove to be a problematic client, fighting his legal counsel every step of the way. It started as early as jury selection, where Oteri wanted to exclude young women who he felt might identify with the victim. Capano, however, insisted on including them, since he was convinced that he could charm them. That says a lot about the narcissistic character of the man, but the real bombshell was still to come.

On October 26, Oteri stunned the courtroom with his opening statement, admitting that Capano had dumped Anne Marie Fahey's body at sea. However, he claimed that her death had been an accident. According to this convoluted version of events, it was Capano's mistress, Deborah MacIntyre, who had shot Anne Marie. MacIntyre had apparently arrived at Capano's home while he was there with Anne Marie and had attacked her rival in a fit of jealous rage. The two had struggled for the gun, which had discharged, hitting Anne Marie in the head and killing her. Capano had disposed of the body in order to protect his lover and his reputation.

That was just the opening salvo in a case that seldom failed to produce fireworks. Capano clashed frequently with prosecutor Colm Connolly and also with his defense team who he threatened to fire at every turn. In the end, however, it was the prosecution's version of events that the jury chose to believe. This was the culmination of some exceptional investigative work by the FBI, and it painted a compelling picture of what had happened to Anne Marie Fahey.

This version held that Capano had been furious over Anne Marie's relationship with Michael Scanlon and her refusal to break it off. He'd decided that if she would not come back to him, he was going to kill her and had convinced Deborah MacIntyre to buy the gun for him for that purpose. The dinner on June 27, 1996, had been Anne Marie's last chance to comply. When she still refused to rekindle their relationship, she unwittingly sealed her own fate. Anne Marie was driven back to Capano's house on some pretense.

There she was shot to death and her body wrapped in a carpet. Later, she was crammed into the plastic cooler box and loaded onto Gerard Capano's fishing boat. She was then taken some 60 miles out to sea and committed to a watery grave. Later, Capano's other brother, Louis, assisted with the cleanup by getting rid of the bloodstained carpet and love seat.

Thomas Capano was found guilty of first-degree murder in January of 1999. He was sentenced to death, although that sentence was later commuted to life in prison. His actual term would amount to a little over 12 years. Capano was found dead in his cell at the Delaware State Prison on September 19, 2011, the victim of a suspected heart attack.

For the Love of God

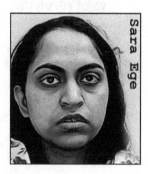

Sara Khan was a bright girl from Hyderabad, India, who excelled at high school and went on to earn a first-class honors degree in mathematics. That should have set her up for a bright future, but to Sara's parents, the idea of their daughter forging a career was of secondary concern. Far more important was marriage. When Sara was 20, they decided that it was time and set about finding a suitable partner for her.

This might seem like a strange concept to someone raised in a Western culture. But in India and Pakistan, it is considered entirely normal. Arranged marriages are common and, in the Muslim faith, it is the responsibility of a young woman's parents to find her a husband. And so, Mohamed Ali Khan and his wife Nafees registered Sara with a marriage broker and were soon presented with the credentials of a potential suitor.

On paper, Yousuf Ali Ege seemed the ideal match for Sara. He was young, ambitious and educated, having earned a Master's degree

from the University of Cardiff. He was also on an upward
trajectory in his career. At the age of 26, he was the manager of a
large branch of The Royal Mail in Cardiff, Wales. To the Kahns,
these were impressive credentials indeed. Within days of receiving
Yousuf's information from the agency, they had agreed to meet
with his parents. Days later, having just met her new husband for
the first time, Sara Kahn was exchanging vows with him. Two days
after that, she was on a flight to the UK, a country she'd never
visited before.

But, as Sara was soon to find out, she and her parents had been
duped. Yousuf did not have a Master's degree; he'd hardly finished
high school. And he was not the manager of the Royal Mail branch;
he worked there as a delivery driver. He also had a night-time job
as a taxi driver and was seldom home. That, perhaps, was a
blessing in disguise because Yousuf was a brutal man who beat
and humiliated his new bride. Sara, alone in a foreign country
without the support of friends and family, became desperately
lonely and unhappy. Still, it was unthinkable for her to walk out on
her marriage. That would bring shame and dishonor on her family.

One particular bone of contention in the marriage was Sara's
inability to give Yousuf the son he so desperately wanted. Over the
first few years, she suffered several miscarriages and thereafter
could not seem to fall pregnant. Eventually, the desperate couple
sought medical help, and Sara was given IVF treatment. By that
method, she conceived a son, Yaseen, in 2003.

Yousuf was overjoyed at the birth of his son. But his joy was not
out of parental love but rather out of the honor he felt Yaseen

could bring to him. From the very day of the boy's birth, Yousuf informed Sara that their son would be a Hafiz, someone who has memorized the whole of the Koran.

This is an extremely demanding course of study. The Koran has 114 chapters, containing 6,236 verses. It is around 80,000 words long. The process of memorization generally takes between 3 and 6 years, with tuition usually beginning in childhood. It requires long hours of study at a madrasah (a special Islamic school). The pay-off is the reverence afforded to both the Hafiz and his family by the community.

Yaseen, however, did not appear to be a natural at the memorization game. Over the years that followed, neighbors noticed that he often had cuts and bruises on his body. This became even more evident once the boy started school and teachers noticed the injuries. On one occasion, Sara was summoned to speak to the head teacher after Yaseen showed up with a badly bruised hand. Questioned about the injury, Sara admitted that she had hit him with a ruler because he'd been "naughty." The teacher then warned her that corporal punishment of children was illegal and might land her in trouble with the police and Social Services. However, he opted not to report the incident.

And so, the abuse continued. Another time, Yaseen arrived at school and was unable to sit due to severe bruising to his buttocks. Although he refused to say how he had sustained the injuries, teachers assumed that he'd received a beating at home. Sara, however, insisted that he'd hurt himself in a fall. A short while later, she moved Yaseen to a different school.

Then came the night of July 12, 2010, when a 999 dispatcher in Cardiff received a call from a hysterical woman screaming that her house was on fire with her 7-year-old son trapped inside. Firefighters rushed to the scene and quickly got the blaze under control. They then entered the house and found the badly burned body of Yaseen Ege. CPR was immediately applied, but it was clear that the boy was already dead. Something bothered the firefighters, though. There was no soot in the child's mouth which there would surely have been had he breathed in the toxic fumes. The body was also rigid, which was unusual given the circumstances.

Sara Ege was transported to St. David's Hospital for treatment of smoke inhalation. Yaseen was taken there also, although he was pronounced dead on arrival. At this point, it was thought to be a terrible tragedy. Yaseen should not even have been home when the fire started. According to his father, he'd stayed home from school because his class had arranged a "Teddy Bear's Picnic" and Yaseen did not have a teddy bear. Yousuf, medical staff noticed, did not appear particularly distraught at his son's death.

However, the matter would take a shocking new turn once a postmortem was carried out on Yaseen's body. The examination revealed, first of all, that there was no smoke in the child's lungs, a clear indication that he was already dead by the time the fire started. There were other surprises too. Yaseen had suffered a catalogue of injuries to his abdomen and had broken ribs and a fractured arm and finger. These injuries, according to the pathologist, suggested prolonged and systematic abuse.

And who might have inflicted these injuries? There were only two suspects – the boy's parents. Brought in for questioning, Yousuf not only denied hurting his son, he denied even knowing about the injuries. Sara was more forthcoming. She admitted that it was she who had killed the boy, although she claimed that it had not been deliberate. According to her, Yaseen's Koran studies were going badly and she had beaten him to motivate his learning. That beating had gone too far. "I couldn't stop myself," she said. "I lost control."

Sara Ege would later attempt to retract her confession but was nonetheless charged with murder. Her husband was charged with causing or allowing the death of his son by failing to act. The couple was tried together, appearing at Cardiff Crown Court in May 2012. There, Sara's taped confession was the key piece of evidence against them. It made for harrowing listening in the hushed courtroom.

Sara is heard admitting on tape that she regularly beat her 7-year-old son with a stick over his failure to learn the Koran. "I beat him like a dog," she said. "But he was so good and never complained." On the day of Yaseen's death, she had beaten him so viciously that he had eventually collapsed to the floor, still murmuring tracts from the Koran. She had then dragged him to the kitchen where she gave him a glass of milk to drink. However, he was shaking and spilled milk on his clothes. She then sent him to his bedroom to change. When he failed to return, she assumed that he'd fallen asleep. However, when she went to check on him 10 minutes later, she found him lying on the floor, shivering and shaking. He gulped "one final breath" before dying, she said.

According to Sara, she panicked once she realized that her son was dead. His body was covered in bruises, so it would be clear to anyone that he had suffered severe physical abuse. She had then decided to hide these injuries by pouring lighter fluid over the body and setting it alight.

That, at least, was the story that Sara Ege told just after her arrest. Now, her defense attorney offered a different one to the court. It was not Sara who had killed Yaseen, he said, it was Yousuf. According to this version of events, Sara had been a victim of physical abuse throughout her marriage. She had made numerous visits to the emergency room of her local hospital during that time (proof of this was entered into evidence). Yousuf had also beaten his son regularly, usually over his problems with learning the Koran. When Sara threatened to report him to the authorities, Yousuf had challenged her to do so, saying that it would result in their son being taken away by Social Services. It was this which prevented her from reporting the abuse.

On the day of the murder, Yousuf had again beaten their son. According to Sara, he had punched the boy repeatedly in the stomach, causing internal injuries which ultimately led to his death. "I loved Yaseen very much," she said. "I would never have done anything to hurt him."

But the question this raised was obvious. Why, then, had she confessed? Sara had an answer for that, too. She said that Yousuf's family had visited her family in India and had threatened to kill them if any harm befell him. It was to protect them that she had given her false confession to the police.

Yousuf's attorney, of course, dismissed this defense. He also reiterated his client's claim that he knew nothing about the abuse. "Mr. Ege worked two jobs," he said, "and was seldom home. Since his son never complained and since he assumed that his wife was a caring and devoted mother, he never suspected the violence that was being inflicted on the boy."

This was clearly a lie. Yaseen's injuries were so severe, it would have been impossible not to notice. In the end, though, the jury found it just too difficult to decide which of these conflicted stories was true. After three days of deliberation, they returned to say that they were unable to reach a verdict. The judge then had no option but to declare a mistrial.

The second trial, starting on October 31, 2012, was a near mirror image of the first – with a few notable exceptions. This time the prosecution leaned heavily on the fact that Sara had given the police four different versions of events. The implication was clear. She had lied then and was probably lying now. Prosecutor Ian Murphy also got Sara to admit on the stand that she had been angry at her son and frustrated by his failure to learn the Koran.

And that admission turned out to be crucial. On December 5, 2012, the jury deliberated for eight hours before returning a unanimous verdict of guilty against Sara Ege. Yousuf, meanwhile, was found not guilty on all charges, a verdict that was treated with outrage, particularly among women's groups. He walked from the courtroom without showing a modicum of emotion.

Sara Ege was sentenced to life in prison, with a minimum term of 17 years before she can apply for parole. While many commentators consider this (and Yousuf's acquittal) a travesty of justice, it should not be forgotten who the real victim is. At the heart of this case is the senseless death of an innocent little boy whose only crime was his failure to memorize some ancient religious tracts.

Heartless

On the morning of Monday, 22 January, 2006, the doorbell rang at the home of Clifford and Yvonne Entwistle in Worksop, England. Yvonne answered it and was shocked to find her son Neil on the doorstep. Neil had moved to America with his wife Rachel and baby daughter, Lillian Rose, just six months earlier. He'd given no indication to his parents that he'd be returning to England anytime soon. One look at Neil's face, though, told Yvonne that this was no ordinary visit. He looked bewildered, on the verge of a breakdown. "What is it, son?" a concerned Yvonne asked. "Rach is dead," Neil blurted out. "Lilly is dead. They've been shot."

Cliff and Yvonne could barely believe what they were hearing. Their daughter-in-law dead? Their beloved granddaughter dead? Who would have done such a thing? It did not even enter their minds for a moment that it might be their son. Neil was devoted to his family. But as deep as their pain ran, the nightmare for the Entwistles was only just beginning. To their grief would soon be added another layer of torment when Neil was arrested, extradited back to America, placed on trial for the murders of the wife and daughter he claimed to love.

Neil Entwistle was born in Nottingham, England on September 18, 1978, and was the older of Cliff and Yvonne Entwistle's two sons. He grew up to be an active and athletic child who loved Cub Scouts and playing soccer. He was also an intelligent boy who did well at school and was eventually accepted at York University. It was there that he met Rachel Souza, an American studying in the UK. Drawn together by their mutual love of rowing, Neil and Rachel soon began dating. They married after graduation in August 2003, and set up home in Droitwich, Worcestershire where Neil found a job working for a tech company and Rachel taught high school. The couple appeared to have a very close relationship and did everything together. When their daughter, Lillian Rose, arrived in April 2005, they could not have been happier.

Cliff and Yvonne were also delighted at the arrival of their first grandchild. They doted on the little girl and looked forward to watching her grow and to being a part of her life. But when Lilly was three months old, the elder Entwistles received disappointing news. Neil and Rachel had decided to move back to Rachel's hometown in Massachusetts. It was a bitter disappointment but one that Cliff and Yvonne accepted with good grace. Little did they know that when they bid a tearful goodbye to Lilly in July 2005 that they would never see their much-loved granddaughter again.

Life back in the States was tough for Neil and Rachel. Initially, they moved in with Rachel's mother and stepfather, Priscilla and Joe Matterazzo, in Carver, Massachusetts. But Joe was a difficult man to live with. The baby's crying seemed to annoy him. So too did Neil's difficulty in finding a job and the continued presence of house guests in his home. Perhaps feeling unwelcome, Rachel sank into a deep depression. She seemed perpetually close to tears and forever tired. Seeking to remedy the situation, Neil dipped into the couple's savings and rented a home for them. Since neither of them was working at the time, this was a risky move. Neil made it more so by his ostentatious choice of residence, a four-bedroom colonial with a price tag of $2,700 per month. Then he placed further strain on their finances by hiring a $400-a-month BMW SUV.

And that was just the start of the spending spree. Soon Neil was maxing out the couple's 18 credit cards on furnishings for their new home. It was foolhardy in the extreme, and it did nothing to lift Rachel out of her funk. She remained deeply unhappy, and perhaps postnatal depression was not the only reason. Perhaps it had something to do with her husband's growing obsession with pornography. Neil was by now trawling the web nightly, visiting sites like Adult Friend Finder, Naughty Nightlife and Hot Local Escorts. These are not just porn sites but also offered "adult hook-ups" and escort services. Neil Entwistle had even posted a profile, accompanied by a semi-nude picture of himself.

We will never know if Entwistle ever cheated on his wife with anyone he met on these sites, just as we will never know with absolute certainty whether he murdered his wife and daughter. What we do know is that when Rachel's friend visited her at home on Friday, January 20, her knock went unanswered. We know also that Rachel was due to meet her mother for lunch that day and failed to show. Both women phoned the police, and a cruiser was dispatched to check on the Entwistle residence. The two officers who entered the home reported that they found nothing untoward. They simply had not looked hard enough.

By the following morning, Priscilla Matterazzo was frantic with worry. She had spent the night desperately calling Rachel and Neil but had received no reply. Again she phoned the police and again they sent a cruiser to the Entwistle residence. This time, the officers noticed a foul odor immediately on entering the house. Rachel and Lilly were found lying side by side under the blankets of the unmade bed. Rachel had been shot in the head. The front of the baby's pajamas was caked with dried blood, indicating that she had been shot in the abdomen.

But where was Neil Entwistle? The Massachusetts State Police started making inquiries and soon learned that Entwistle had flown out of Logan International Airport on January 21, bound for London on a one-way ticket. An officer then called his parents' home and was surprised to get Entwistle on the phone. He was even more surprised when Entwistle told him that he knew about the deaths of his wife and daughter.

According to Entwistle, he had left the house early on Friday morning to do some shopping. When he returned, he found both Rachel and Lilly shot to death. He'd been so distraught that he'd gone downstairs to fetch a kitchen knife to kill himself. However, he'd lacked the courage to go through with it. He'd then decided to drive to his in-laws' house to tell his mother-in-law what had happened. On the way there, he remembered that Joe Matterazzo had a .22 pistol and decided that he could use that to commit suicide. However, no one was home when he arrived, and the house was securely locked. He'd decided then that he needed to get home to see his parents and had driven to Logan airport. He admitted to the officer that he'd probably acted foolishly and should have called 911 after finding the bodies.

Entwistle's story sounded highly unlikely. In fact, he was immediately elevated to the top of the suspect list. Over the days that followed, that suspicion would be backed up as the police uncovered considerable evidence against Entwistle. First there was his rental vehicle, found abandoned at Logan airport. Inside, detectives found Entwistle's laptop computer containing some interesting insights into the character of the man. There was proof of his prodigious porn consumption, as well as evidence of fraud. Entwistle had been running a scam on eBay, selling bogus computer equipment. His inbox contained scores of emails from disgruntled customers, claiming that they had not received the goods they'd paid for. Even more damaging were the internet searches that Entwistle had done in the days leading up to the murder. One of those was "how to kill someone with a knife."

It also became clear very early on that Entwistle had lied about his visit to the Matterazzo residence. He'd said that he hadn't been able to get in, but Priscilla Matterazzo told police that he had a key to the premises. And the reason behind that lie was soon evident. Forensics proved that Joe Matterazzo's .22 Colt had fired the fatal shots. Investigators now believed that Entwistle had removed the gun from the premises, used it to kill his wife and daughter and then returned it to its original place.

While all of this was going on, Entwistle was holed up at his parents' home in Worksop, with the world's media camped outside. He would remain there until February 9, 2006, when two of his old university buddies convinced him to join them on a trip to London to escape the constant media spotlight. Unbeknownst to Entwistle, he was under police surveillance from the moment he left the house. As he stepped from a tube train at London's Royal Oak station, officers stepped forward and arrested him.

Entwistle's lawyers initially indicated that he intended fighting extradition to the United States. However, within a day of his arrest, he changed his mind and signed a waiver. Within days, he was on a flight back to America, bound for a Massachusetts courtroom.

In the eyes of the American public and media, Entwistle had already been declared guilty. But by the time the matter came to trial, Entwistle and his defense team had put together an interesting case, one that, at the very least, muddied the waters. Entwistle now claimed that it was Rachel who had shot Lilly before turning the gun on herself. He'd found the two of them dead in the bedroom and had removed the gun from Rachel's hand and returned it to her parents' home. He'd done it, he said, because he wanted to spare Rachel from the "shame and humiliation" of the crime she'd committed. As for motive, he ventured that it was Rachel's postnatal depression that had driven her to murder.

On the surface, this seems to be a fanciful and self-serving explanation. But the defense team had done their homework. On the stand, they got detectives to admit that they had never considered the possibility of a murder/suicide; they got a forensics expert to concede that gunshot residue had been found on Rachel's hands and that none had been found on the steering wheel of Entwistle's SUV; they got a psychologist to testify that postnatal depression might have been a motive.

Unfortunately for the defense, the jury rejected this theory. It is easy to see why. Entwistle had appeared cold and disinterested throughout most of the trial, just what you'd expect from a heartless monster who had shot his own 9-month-old daughter; his portrayal as a pornography-obsessed pervert and an internet fraudster spoke of a man with few scruples; his internet searches proved that he was, at least, thinking about killing his family. And if his murder/suicide story was true, why hadn't he called 911 as any rational person would have done? Why had he fled? Aside from all that, there was the murder weapon which he had access to and his prints on said weapon. It all added up to a compelling case for murder. It was no surprise to anyone when the jury returned a verdict of guilty.

Neil Entwistle was sentenced to life in prison without the possibility of parole. He is currently held at the Old Colony Correctional Center in Bridgewater, Massachusetts, where he spends much of his time in solitary confinement for his own protection.

Three Into Two Won't Go

Thomas Dixon

Dr. Joseph Sonnier was the personification of the American dream. Raised dirt-poor in South Dakota, he had gone on to graduate at the top of his class at high school, to college and medical school, and had a successful pathology practice in Lubbock, Texas. Along the way, the doctor had acquired a reported fortune of around $12 million and a love of international travel and fine wines. The only blot on this otherwise perfect life was the breakdown of his marriage to his high school sweetheart, Becky Gallegos. Becky had left him for another man in 2001, after a 27-year marriage that had produced two sons. She would be murdered by her new husband in July 2010, a tragedy that deeply affected Dr. Sonnier.

The Sonniers had divorced in 2003, leaving Joseph, then aged 48, heartbroken and at somewhat of a loose end. He'd wed Becky right out of school and had known nothing but married life throughout his adulthood. Now single for the first time in nearly 30 years, Sonnier decided to make a fresh start by moving to Lubbock, Texas. Keen to make connections in his new home, he took the advice of one of his sons and signed up for a ballroom dancing class. That was where he met Richelle Shetina, a beautiful, twice-married mother of four. She and Dr. Sonnier hit it off almost immediately and were soon an item, vacationing together in California and in Paris, France. There is some dispute over whether marriage plans were ever discussed. Dr. Sonnier was apparently against the idea, even though he and Richelle were devoted to one another.

Then, on July 10, 2012, almost two years to the day after his former wife had been murdered, Dr. Sonnier's gilded life all came crashing down. That was the day that the doctor arrived home to find a man sitting on a chair in his backyard. Sonnier didn't recognize the man, so he knocked on a window to draw his attention. Then, as the man got up and started walking towards him, he opened the window a crack and asked what he was doing in his yard. To his surprise, the man suddenly produced a gun from the paper bag he was carrying and fired twice, hitting the doctor in the chest and shoulder.

Sonnier reeled back, bleeding from a couple of bullet wounds. Then he turned and staggered down the passage into the house. The shooter, meanwhile, had forced the window, nearly dislodging it from its frame. He climbed through and followed the trail of blood all the way into the garage. It was there that he found Dr. Sonnier, lying face down on the concrete floor, mortally wounded. The man then drew the second weapon he was carrying, a long, wickedly sharp dagger. This he plunged into his victim's back eleven times before fleeing the scene, exiting the same way that he'd entered.

The following day, staff at Dr. Sonnier's pathology clinic were worried when he didn't show up for work. By mid-morning, having been unable to raise a reply from either the doctor's landline or cellphone, one of his staffers, Mary Rodrigues, decided to drive to his house to check on him. She arrived to find landscapers working in the front yard and asked for their help. Together, the three of them walked to the rear of the house where they found the damaged window as well as a shell casing lying on the floor. Rodrigues and one of the landscapers then entered the home and soon found Dr. Sonnier lying on the floor of the garage in a pool of blood. They immediately called 911.

Within minutes, several police cruisers had pulled up in front of the Sonnier residence and officers had started to cordon off the area. Then detectives and crime scene technicians moved in to look for evidence. They found blood spatters and large footprints throughout the house. They also noted that nothing appeared to have been taken, even though there were valuables on display throughout the luxury home. It was clear from the start that this was no botched burglary. This was personal.

But who would have wanted to kill Dr. Sonnier? By all accounts, he was a respected, admired, and well-liked man with no known enemies. Perhaps his girlfriend, Richelle, would be able to shed some light.

Richelle Shetina was quite obviously devastated by the loss of the man she described as "the love of my life." But she had something else to share with investigators. In the weeks leading up to Dr. Sonnier's murder, she said that she had become aware of someone stalking her. Asked if she had any idea who that might be, she offered up the name of her ex-boyfriend, Dr. Thomas Dixon.

Dixon was a plastic surgeon who ran a very successful cosmetology clinic in Amarillo, Texas. Richelle had met him when she'd started attending the clinic for Botox treatments. Dixon had been married at the time, but he and Richelle soon became involved in a steamy affair, leading to the break-up of the doctor's marriage. But Dixon's relationship with Richelle hadn't stood the test of time. She described it as volatile and said that they had mutually decided to call it quits after 18 months. Shortly after, Richelle had met Dr. Sonnier and they had started dating. According to Richelle, that had made her ex angry.

The following day, July 12, two Lubbock PD investigators traveled the 100 miles to Amarillo to question Dr. Dixon. They found him at home with his girlfriend, Ashley, a medical intern half his age. Dixon willingly allowed the officers in and offered no objection when they asked if they could question him and Ashley separately. Under interrogation, he admitted that he still loved Richelle but insisted that he hadn't seen her nor spoken to her in months. He conceded that he was unhappy with Richelle dating another man but denied any involvement in Dr. Sonnier's death. At the time of the murder, he said, he'd been right here in Amarillo, having dinner with Ashley.

Ashley's version of events supported Dr. Dixon's story. She did, however, include one small detail which he'd failed to mention. On the day of the murder, Dixon had been visited by a friend named David Shepard, and the two had spoken privately in the study.

Asked about this, Dixon said that he recalled the visit but said that it had been nothing important. Shepard had just come over to pick up some cigars. The officers accepted that explanation and left.

The following day, a Lubbock detective phoned David Shepard and asked about his whereabouts on the day of the murder. Shepard provided an alibi, claiming he'd been at home in Amarillo, but his nervous demeanor gave the detective cause to wonder whether he was being truthful. Still, with nothing to disprove his story, the cops were forced to let it drop. They did, however, do some checking into Shepard's background and found that he was known in Amarillo as a bit of a braggart who like to spin tall tales hinting at his dark past. Those stories were likely a lie, since Shepard did not have a police record. Investigators also noted that Shepard was a huge man, standing over six-foot-five and heavily built. He could easily be a match for the large footprints found in Dr. Sonnier's home.

Days passed with no significant progress in the investigation. Then, on July 14, the police caught an unexpected break when they got a call from a man named Paul Reynolds. Reynolds was an army veteran, now working as a registered nurse at an Amarillo hospital. He was a childhood friend of Dave Shepard and was currently sleeping on the couch at his buddy's home. And he had an interesting tale to tell. According to Reynolds, Shepard was having a breakdown of sorts and had twice attempted suicide. The reason? Shepard had confided in him that he'd killed "some doctor in Lubbock."

Reynolds said that Shepard had admitted killing the Lubbock doctor in exchange for $9,000, paid by a buddy of his. As far as Reynolds had been able to discern, the doctor had been dating the former girlfriend of Shepard's buddy, and the man wanted to get rid of him. Shepard had apparently been stalking the doctor for weeks before he eventually struck, shooting and stabbing his victim to death. This, of course, matched the situation surrounding Joseph Sonnier. Sonnier had been dating Richelle Shetina, the ex-girlfriend of Dr. Thomas Dixon, and Dixon had admitted to police that he still had feelings for her. That would make Dixon the man who'd hired Shepard to carry out the hit.

On July 16, both Dixon and Shepard were taken into custody and charged with first-degree murder, with indictments later affirmed by a grand jury. But there was still a case to prove and, particularly in the case of Thomas Dixon, that case was far from clear cut. Then, in October 2012, all of that changed when Shepard contacted prosecutors and said that he needed to talk to them.

Shepard told investigators that he wanted to clear his conscience and was prepared to tell them everything. According to him, Dixon had asked for his help in winning back Richelle Shetina. The original idea had been to cause problems in her relationship with Joseph Sonnier by making it appear that Sonnier was being unfaithful. First, they tried to recruit a woman who would be prepared to say that she'd slept with Sonnier while he was dating Shetina. When that failed, they wrote a letter to Shetina, purportedly from a woman named Tina. In it, "Tina" claimed that she had agreed to sleep with Dr. Sonnier for money and was angry because the doctor hadn't paid her. She was writing to Richelle to let her know what kind of a man she was involved with.

Dr. Sonnier, of course, denied the accusation posed in the letter. And he was believed by Richelle. Dixon's plan to split up the couple had failed. Now it was time to move on to more drastic action, action that would ultimately end in the murder of Dr. Joseph Sonnier. According to Shepard, he had gone along with it because he didn't want to let his friend down. He hadn't realized how difficult it would be to deal with the consequences of what he'd done.

David Shepard would ultimately accept a plea bargain, pleading guilty in 2013, in exchange for a life sentence. Dixon, meanwhile, decided to take his chances with a jury. He maintained that he'd never asked Shepard to commit murder and that Shepard had acted on his own. But if that was the case, how had Shepard come into possession of the murder weapon, a .25-caliber pistol registered to Dixon's brother? Why had the doctor paid Shepard $9,000? And what possible motive could Shepard have had to murder a man who was a complete stranger to him?

These were questions that Dixon's defense team could never explain to the satisfaction of the jury. After an initial mistrial, he was found guilty and sentenced to life in prison without the possibility of parole.

The Dominici Affair

It was the French Emperor Napoleon who famously quipped that
"an army marches on its stomach." And he would have found a
vocal supporter for that view in Sir Jack Drummond, an eminent
British scientist who was an expert on nutrition and chief scientific
adviser to the Ministry of Food during WWII. It would be no
exaggeration to say that Drummond's groundbreaking work
played a key part in the ultimate victory and in maintaining the
morale of the nation during a time of scarcity and deprivation. It
earned him a knighthood in 1944 and, after the war, a position as
director of research with the pharmaceutical company Boots.

Seven years after the end of the conflict in Europe, Sir Jack was 61
years old and living in Nottingham, England with his wife, Anne,
and the couple's 10-year-old daughter, Elizabeth. In the spring of
1952, he was due to attend a scientific conference in Paris but was
forced to cancel his attendance when he was diagnosed with a
cerebral hemorrhage. A period of recuperation followed but, by
July, Sir Jack was well enough to take up the offer of a vacation on
the French Riviera. He and his family had been invited to stay with

an old friend and colleague, Guy Marrian, professor of biochemistry at Edinburgh University. Professor Marrian owned a villa in Villefranche-sur-Mer, near Nice.

On the morning of Friday, July 25, the Drummonds drove away from their Nottingham home with Sir Jack at the wheel of a new Hillman motor vehicle. Elizabeth Drummond was particularly excited by the family vacation. The ten-year-old was a bright and energetic child, the light of her father's life. In no time at all, she'd drawn up an itinerary of all the places that she wanted to visit, leaving her father to comment wryly that they would require several months to complete the list.

After a stop off in London, the family traveled to Dover and took the ferry from there to Dunkirk, arriving on Monday, July 28. From there, they drove to Reims and Domrémy, where Elizabeth wanted to visit the birthplace of Joan of Arc. After stopping in Aix-les-Bains, they pushed on to Digne. There, Elizabeth saw a poster for a charlottade de corso – a bullfight in which the bull is not killed. It was scheduled for the coming Monday, and Elizabeth begged her parents to bring her back to see it. As always when it came to his daughter, Sir Jack agreed and booked tickets for the event. He then drove on to Villefranche, where the Drummonds spent a pleasant weekend with Professor Marrian and his family.

On Monday, August 4, the Drummonds were on their way back to Digne, leaving their passports and most of their valuables at the villa. The corso was every bit as thrilling as Elizabeth had hoped it would be. After it concluded, the family had drinks at a cafe before leaving Digne at around 7 p.m. They planned to return to

Villefranche via a circuitous route, taking the N96 Marseille trunk road and camping by the roadside overnight. It was a glorious evening for it, warm and clear with a million stars decorating the heavens.

At about 6 a.m. the following morning, a factory worker named Jean-Marie Olivier was driving home along the N96 after completing his night shift. Olivier had just rounded a bend in the road when a young man ran in front of his vehicle, waving his hands in an agitated fashion. Olivier recognized him. It was Gustave Dominici, whose family had a small farm nearby. "I've just seen a dead body over there," Gustave said breathlessly, pointing towards the river. "There were shots in the night. Fetch the gendarmes."

It took the police an hour to arrive on the scene and mere minutes to realize that this was not a single homicide. This was a massacre. The bullet-riddled body of a man lay on the grass verge to one side of the road. On the other side stood a green estate car, its contents strewn across the ground. Lying face down by the car was a middle-aged woman, partially covered with a blanket. She, too, had been shot several times. The most tragic find was yet to come, though. About 85 yards from the car, in a copse of trees by the riverbank, lay the body of a little girl, dressed in pajamas, her head a bloody mass of gore, brain matter and splintered bone. It appeared that she had tried to flee the attackers and had been run to ground and beaten to death.

Based on the registration plates of the vehicle, the victims were soon identified as Sir Jack Drummond, Lady Drummond, and their daughter, Elizabeth. While the bodies were being removed for autopsy, the police got to work questioning the locals. Their first stop was at the nearby Dominici farm, where 75-year-old Gaston Dominici was patriarch of a 28-strong clan.

Unfortunately, none of the Dominicis had much to share about the night's events. They said that they had seen the family stop their car in the layby at around 8 p.m. and had judged from the vehicle's license plate that they were English. By 10 p.m., all of the Dominicis were abed, only to be woken at about 1 a.m. by the sound of gunshots. None of them paid the gunfire much mind, they said, because there were a number of poachers operating in the area, and they often heard shots at night. They only realized what had happened when Gustave went out into the fields at around 5:30 and discovered the child's body by the river bank. According to Gaston, he only heard about the murder at around 8 a.m. when his son told him about it.

The paucity of information that the police were able to glean from the Dominici family was a disappointment. But it was only the first in a series of setbacks. This investigation would be badly botched, rapidly descending into a farce worthy of Inspector Clouseau. The first problem was assigning a detective to the case. The police department in Nice said that it was too understaffed to spare an investigator, while the Marseille CID claimed that most of its investigators were on holiday. Eventually, after a 24-hour delay, Superintendent Sebeille was dispatched from Marseille. He immediately made a cardinal blunder, failing to seal off the area and allowing reporters, photographers and even onlookers to traipse through the crime scene. Footprints were trampled on, fingerprints smudged, crucial evidence handled. Several items, including a strip of flesh preserved for forensic examination, went missing.

Amazingly, given the chaotic nature of the investigation, there was a breakthrough on day two when the police found the broken stock and barrel of a rifle. A bloodstained chip of wood found near Elizabeth Drummond's body exactly matched a piece missing from the stock, marking this out as the weapon used to bludgeon the little girl to death. Moreover, the gun barrel was covered in grease, meaning there was a strong possibility that fingerprints could be lifted from it. Unfortunately, the police allowed bystanders to handle the weapon, rendering it useless as evidence. Even the bloodstained wood chip disappeared.

And then there was the probable murder weapon, found lying on the ground near the Drummonds' car. It was a US-made semi-automatic M1 carbine. This was a surprisingly common firearm in France during the 1950s. It had been a favorite of the Resistance during the war, and now just about every peasant family owned one. Everyone, it seems, except for the Dominicis, all of whom claimed that they had never even seen an M1, let alone handled one.

Those denials served only to arouse Superintendent Sebeille's suspicions. From the very start, he had believed that someone from the Dominici farm was involved. And those suspicions were only deepened when inconsistencies began to creep into their statements. Gaston Dominici swore that his family had had no contact with the Drummonds. Yet, according to his 17-year-old grandson, the English family had called at the farm asking for water. Gaston had also spoken out of turn while being questioned by the police. He had told them that Lady Drummond had "died instantly." How could he possibly have known that unless he had been involved in her death?

With the murder case now attracting massive media attention, a sub-plot began to emerge, particularly in the more left-leaning French newspapers. It was a story of police prejudice against the Dominici clan. According to this narrative, the police wanted to solve the murder of a prominent British peer as quickly as possible and had therefore decided to scapegoat a poor peasant family, twisting the evidence to achieve that goal. In truth, though, the Dominicis did themselves few favors. They were often uncooperative, and when they did answer questions, they were prone to making incriminating statements.

First there was the admission that Elizabeth had still been alive when Gustave found her. That resulted in his arrest and subsequent two months' imprisonment for "failing to give assistance to a person in mortal peril." Then, in November 1953, came the revelation that everyone on the Dominici farm had heard screams and gunfire and that Gustave had tampered with the crime scene before flagging down Jean-Marie Olivier. Later, Gustave and his elder brother, Clovis, independently admitted that their father had come into the house just after 1 a.m. on August 5 and had declared: "I have killed the English."

Gaston Dominici was promptly arrested, eliciting a fury of lurid reportage from the country's newspapers. "Monster of Lurs Unmasked," read one of the headlines, although the 75-year-old

Gaston hardly looked the part. And there should have been serious doubts raised about the confession he gave to the police. It sounded more like an old man's sexual fantasy than an actual admission of murder.

According to Gaston, he had crept up on the Drummonds' campsite during the night and had observed Lady Drummond undressing. He had become sexually aroused and had therefore approached and propositioned her. They had started having sex, but then Sir Jack woke up and angrily confronted him. A struggle had then ensued over Gaston's gun, during which Sir Jack was shot through the hand. Gaston had then fled but had turned and fired twice from the roadside, in order to silence Lady Drummond who was screaming. He'd then noticed the child fleeing towards the river and had given chase. Since he had by now used up all of his bullets, he'd killed her with a "single blow" of the rifle butt.

Even ignoring the preposterous notion of the sexual encounter, there were major problems with Gaston's story. No burn marks were found on Sir Jack's hand, which there would have been if he'd been shot at while holding the rifle barrel; Lady Drummond was shot three times, whereas Gaston claimed to have fired twice; and Elizabeth sustained several blows to the forehead, not the single blow Gaston claims to have inflicted. It is also unlikely that Gaston, who walked with a cane, could have caught up with a fleet-footed 10-year-old, fleeing in terror. In any case, Gaston later withdrew his confession, hinting that he'd only made it to protect others in his family (by implication Gustave) and to "safeguard the honor of his grandchildren."

Throughout 1954, Gaston gave several confessions which he then promptly withdrew. Gustave, meanwhile, had retracted his statement about his father returning at 1 a.m. in the morning and claiming he'd "shot the English." Gaston's older son, Clovis, however, was adamant that Gaston had spoken those words after returning from his late night ramble. It was largely on the basis of this statement that Gaston Dominici was hauled before the courts at the Palais de Justice in Digne on November 17, 1954.

In truth, the prosecution case was exceedingly weak, its evidence tainted, based on hearsay and the utterings of an old man who was clearly not in possession of all his faculties. But Gaston was poorly represented, and the evidence against him deemed sufficient to find him guilty. After an 11-day trial, he was sentenced to execution by guillotine. That sentence was later commuted to life in prison with hard labor, although Gaston would remain behind bars for less than six years before being released in 1960 on grounds of ill health. He died in 1965, aged 88, at a hospice in Digne.

But was justice really served in the Affaire' Dominici? There are many who believe that Gaston was railroaded, a convenient fall guy to cover up a seriously botched investigation of a high-profile case. Gaston, himself, hinted that his son, Gustave, might have been involved while recently uncovered evidence points to a different suspect (or suspects) altogether.

It has been reported that a German criminal, Wilhelm Bartkowski, part of a violent, multi-national gang of four, admitted to being involved in the murders after he was arrested on unrelated

charges in November 1952. According to Bartkowski, he and his
accomplices had driven to France to carry out a jewel heist in
Marseille. They had encountered the Drummonds camping by the
roadside and had decided on a whim to murder and rob them. This
story was affirmed by Bartkowski's three accomplices after they
were arrested in April 1965. These confessions were, apparently,
forwarded to the French authorities who decided not to take any
action. Gaston, they reasoned, had done his time and been
released. No point in opening up old wounds.

In France today, you will find few commentators who believe that
Gaston Dominici was guilty. Most consider the outcome to be a
major miscarriage of justice. The case, meanwhile, has inspired
articles, books, films, documentaries and investigative websites.
Perhaps someday, one of those will provide the definitive answer
to this enduring mystery.

Happy Never After

The cast seems bland enough, a pair of high school teachers, one recently divorced and needy in love, the other a tweed-wearing English major. Add to that a high school principal who had once been an Air Force colonel and now brought his own peculiar brand of governance to Upper Merion Area High School in King of Prussia, Pennsylvania. These were hardly the sort of people you'd expect to find embroiled in a sensational murder case. Scratch below the surface, though, and a whole new world emerges, one of serial philandering, fraud and robbery; one of Satanism, sex parties, bestiality, and murder.

It started when 36-year-old Susan Reinert moved to Pennsylvania to take up a teaching position at Upper Merion High. Susan's marriage had recently ended in divorce, and she had gained custody of her two children, Karen, 11, and Michael, aged 10. In Pennsylvania, she found a chance to start again, a new job and a modest but tidy home on Woodcrest Avenue, Ardmore. There Susan intended putting her life, all of their lives, back together again.

Whether or not romance figured in those plans is not known. Nonetheless, it soon put in an appearance in the form of William Bradfield, a fellow English teacher at Upper Merion. Blue-eyed and bearded, Bradfield was not a conventionally handsome man. He did, however, possess a brand of magnetism that appeared to draw women to him. Susan Reinert was no exception. Shortly after starting her tenure at the school, she and Bradfield were an item, even though he swore her to silence about the relationship and vehemently denied it whenever he was asked. He had good reason for these vociferous denials. At the time he was dating Susan, Bradfield was also living with another teacher on staff, seeing a former student, and carrying on a sexual relationship with a fourth woman.

Everyone but Susan Reinert seems to have known about Bradfield's duplicitousness. His fellow teachers even joked about "Bradfield's Harem." But Susan was blinded by love, prepared to believe Bradfield's promises that they would soon be married. That proposal turned out to be a prelude to Bradfield's request for a $25,000 loan. According to Bradfield, he had the opportunity to invest in a start-up that would secure their future. Susan barely blinked before writing the check. She then made an even larger financial commitment to Bradfield, designating him as the sole beneficiary of her $730,000 life insurance policy. With the stroke of a pen, she'd disinherited her children in favor of her lover. Although she didn't know it yet, she'd also signed their death warrants.

Aside from his complex web of relationships with women, William Bradfield had one other significant friendship – with Upper Merion High principal, Jay Smith. Smith was an odd (some would say bizarre) character. Many on the school faculty thought he was "creepy," and some called him "the Prince of Darkness" behind his back. Rumors would later emerge that he was a Satanist, that he organized swinging sex parties with other teachers at the school, and that he'd been involved in a number of murders, burning the bodies in the school incinerator. There were stories that he'd done something to accelerate his wife's cancer, leading to her death. He was also suspected in the disappearance of his drug-addict daughter and her husband.

Whether or not those stories were true, Jay Smith was not your typical high school administrator. That much became evident on August 19, 1978, when Smith was arrested while trying to pull off an armed robbery at the Gateway Shopping Center in Chester County. Smith was dressed in a security guard uniform, and he'd come to the mall equipped for all eventualities. Inside his Ford Granada, the police found several loaded handguns, a ski mask, a syringe filled with a tranquilizing drug, and several other items described by police as burglary and robbery tools. Smith tried to explain away the evidence by saying that the guns were needed as protection from people who had been "harassing him." The drugs, he insisted, belonged to his junkie son-in-law.

But Smith had a harder time explaining away the items found in his home – more weapons, more drugs, security-guard uniforms and fake badges, office equipment pilfered from the high school, and four gallons of nitric acid, apparently stolen from the same source. There was also a sizeable collection of illicit pornography, most of it involving bestiality.

Jay Smith was charged with two armed robberies, committed at the Sears stores in St. David's and at the Neshaminy Mall. At his March 1979 trial, William Bradfield appeared as an alibi witness. His testimony was ultimately rejected by the jury, who found Smith guilty as charged. He was released on bond, pending sentencing. He was still out on bail on June 25, 1979, the day that Susan Reinert and her children disappeared.

Susan's body was found that same day, battered and bruised and stuffed into the wheel well of her orange Plymouth Horizon. The car had been left in the parking lot of a Harrisburg hotel, some 90 miles from her home. Cause of death was later determined to be a massive overdose of morphine, probably administered by her killer, since Susan was not a drug user. Susan had not died easily. She had been severely abused before her death. Both of her eyes had been blackened, and there were odd-shaped bruises on her back which suggested that she'd been beaten with a chain. As for her children, they were simply gone, vanished, disappeared.

Over the weeks that followed, pictures of Karen and Michael Reinert were more or less a permanent fixture on the front pages of the local newspapers. In the meanwhile, the police and emergency services conducted a search for the children. Despite their considerable efforts, it came up empty.

So who had killed Susan Reinert and probably also her children? William Bradfield was the most likely suspect since he stood to gain the most from their deaths. Except that Bradfield had an alibi. On the weekend that Susan died and her children disappeared, he'd been at the beach in Cape May, New Jersey. Several of his work colleagues had been there, too, and could vouch for his whereabouts.

So Bradfield hadn't killed Susan, but that didn't mean that he couldn't have contracted someone else to do the job for him. An obvious candidate was Jay Smith. Smith had been due in court in Harrisburg on the day of the murder and had arrived late for his appearance. The courtroom was just a few miles from the hotel parking lot where police were at that very moment finding Susan Reinert's body. Later, when they lifted the corpse from the vehicle for transport to the morgue, they made an interesting discovery. Lying under the body was a comb bearing the insignia of Jay Smith's Army Reserve unit.

But that was not as damning as it at first appeared. It turned out that thousands of the combs had been given out as promotional items. Susan might have received one herself. While the police strongly suspected that Bradfield had arranged the murders of Susan Reinert and her children and that Smith had carried out the killings, they did not have sufficient evidence to charge either man.

They did, however, have enough to charge Bradfield with theft by deception, related to the $25,000 he'd "borrowed" from Susan. Investigators learned that the money had never been invested but had instead been placed in a safe-deposit box by yet another of

Bradfield's mistresses, Wendy Zeigler. The cash had been withdrawn on the day that Susan was found dead. Bradfield had used some of it to take Zeigler on a vacation to Mexico.

Now, however, Bradfield was in custody, charged with fraud. Not that he appeared too worried by his circumstances. While awaiting trial, he filed a claim with the insurance company for the proceeds of Susan's $730,000 life policy. The matter was soon tied up in litigation as Susan's family counter-sued to prevent him benefitting from her death.

And things were about to get even worse for Bradfield. Facing the prospect of jail time, Wendy Ziegler flipped on her lover and struck a deal with prosecutors. She was the key prosecution witness at Bradfield's July 1981 trial. Convicted of fraud, Bradfield was sentenced to two years in jail.

But the investigators in the Susan Reinert murder case were still determined to nail him for her death and for that of her children, whose bodies had still not been found. On April 6, 1983, Bradfield was arrested and charged with three counts of murder.

The case against Bradfield seemed somewhat tenuous. With scant physical evidence, the prosecution's main strategy appeared designed to join Bradfield and Smith in a murder-for-profit conspiracy. Since Smith had not been charged, this seemed a strange approach. Nonetheless, the case was carefully constructed. Of particular interest was testimony by Bradfield and Reinert's former teaching colleagues. Several of them revealed that Bradfield had expressed concern for Susan in the weeks before her death. He'd suggested that Jay Smith was planning to kill her. Why, then, hadn't he warned Susan or gone to the authorities? It was a question that Bradfield's defense team couldn't answer. He, himself, would never get the chance. On the advice of counsel, he did not take the stand.

In the end, the jury decided that there was sufficient evidence to convict William Bradfield of conspiracy to commit murder. On Oct. 28, 1983, he was sentenced to three life terms, to be served consecutively. He would serve out his sentence at Graterford Prison, dying there of a heart attack in January 1998 at the age of 64.

But what of Jay Smith, who many believed was the actual killer? Smith was still serving his sentence for armed robbery when he was arrested and charged with three counts of murder on June 25, 1985, the sixth anniversary of Susan Reinert's death. Smith's defense team sought to shift the blame for the actual murders to Bradfield, ignoring the fact that Bradfield had a cast iron alibi for that time. The ploy would ultimately fail as Smith was found guilty on all charges. One of the key pieces of physical evidence against him was a class pin that had been found in his car. It had belonged to Karen Reinert.

Jay Smith was sentenced to death for the murders, but he would never keep his date with the executioner. While he was imprisoned on death row, his attorney filed an appeal, citing prosecutorial misconduct. The Pennsylvania Supreme Court agreed and, in December 1989, granted Smith a new trial. Then Smith's attorney filed a new motion, now asserting that Smith was exempt from prosecution under the double jeopardy rule. Three years later, the Supreme Court again ruled in Smith's favor.

In late September 1992, having served his time for his armed robbery conviction, Jay Smith walked away from prison a free man. He died of a heart attack in May 2009 at the age of 80. Smith never admitted to the murders of Susan Reinert and her children. The whereabouts of Karen and Michael remain a mystery to this day.

Predator

Victor Farrant was handsome, with a buff physique from his job as a construction laborer. He was charming, with a smooth line of talk that seldom failed to impress the type of women he targeted. These were usually vulnerable, middle-aged divorcees who he found in clubs and wine bars up and down the English south coast. Any woman who fell for his dubious charms would be showered with compliments, gifts, and flowers – at least at first. But they'd soon learn that Farrant was a demanding individual, and his demands were for a submissive sex partner who acquiesced to his every warped whim. It was rape through intimidation, and if intimidation didn't work, Farrant had other tools in his locker. At least one young woman had already found that out to her cost. The teenager had been battered into submission and then subjected to a brutal rape.

Farrant had served eight years of a 12-year sentence for that crime, but in November 1995, he was free again and back in his old routine. The wine bars of the south coast were again his hunting ground; the predator was on the hunt for prey. Ann Fidler would have been better equipped than most for dealing with a man like Farrant. The attractive 43-year-old had once been the madam of an escort agency. These days, however, she worked for herself, entertaining clients at her apartment in Eastleigh, Hampshire.

We can't be sure whether Farrant knew that Ann was a working girl when he picked her up on December 27, 1995. Chances are that he did. Ann had been in the game long enough to make it clear up front that this was a business transaction. Farrant, however, would not have concerned himself with the fee they negotiated. He had no intention of paying it.

Later that evening, Ann Fidler's husband, Brett, returned home to a darkened house. That confused him. Brett was aware that his wife worked as a high-class hooker, but even when she was entertaining a client, Ann never left all of the lights in the house off. The answer to the conundrum was revealed the moment he turned on the kitchen light. There was a woman lying on the floor in a pool of blood, her face so severely battered that at first he did not recognize her as his wife. Ann Fidler was alive, but only just. She was rushed to hospital where doctors performed emergency surgery, a procedure that necessitated the removal of part of her brain. Miraculously, she would eventually recover from her horrific injuries. Perhaps thankfully, she had no recollection of the attack. It would be left to the medical examiner to fill in the horrific details.

Ann Fidler had been attacked with three wine bottles, her assailant picking up a new one each time the one he was using shattered against her skull. She had been bludgeoned with a clothes iron and slashed with a knife. Her killer had then smashed her head against the window of the oven, using such force that the toughened glass shattered. Finally, he'd fled the scene, leaving his victim for dead on the kitchen floor. And Ann would almost certainly have died had her attacker not left her lying on her side against the tumble dryer. Had she been left on her back, she would have drowned on her own blood.

Later, once Victor Farrant was in custody, the police would estimate that he had attacked as many as 50 women across 20 counties, usually complete strangers who he picked up. But not all of these attacks were random. At least one was premeditated. This was the attack on Glenda Hoskins at her home in Port Solent, Portsmouth in February 1996. The 45-year-old divorcee had started dating Farrant after she separated from her husband. However, she had ended the relationship after she learned of Farrant's criminal record.

That had not gone down well with the muscular Farrant. He was apparently livid when he heard that Glenda was seeing someone else, but before he could do anything about it, he was arrested on the rape charge and sent to prison. The years behind bars had done nothing to quell his lust for revenge. He'd even boasted to fellow inmates that he was going to "teach the bitch a lesson" once he was released. On February 7, 1996, he made good on that promise.

On the afternoon of that day, Glenda's 15-year-old daughter Kate became concerned when her mother did not pick her up from school as arranged. She phoned her father, Tony, and the two of them went to the house together. Having found indications there that something was amiss, Tony called the police and he and an officer carried out a thorough search of the property, including an inspection of the loft. When Kate asked if she could help, Tony suggested that she go through the loft again. He knew, after all, that there was nothing there. The last thing he wanted was for his teenaged daughter to find something that might traumatize her.

But Kate had only been in the loft a few minutes when a blood-curdling scream sent Tony and the police officer rushing to her aid. As Tony scrambled up the ladder into the loft, he saw Kate standing over the nude body of her mother. Glenda had been in the loft all along, her corpse rolled up in a carpet.

The inquiry into Glenda Hoskins's murder was soon in full flow. Crime scene tape was strung, and detectives and CSIs descended on the house. The pathologist's report provided the first indication of just how depraved this murder had been. Glenda had been drowned, and bruises on her ankles suggested that her killer had placed her in the bathtub and then forced her head underwater by pulling her legs up in the air. This was a similar method of murder to that used by the infamous "Brides in the Bath" serial killer, George Joseph Smith.

It also did not take long for the police to identify a suspect. Victor Farrant's fingerprints were all over the crime scene, and as a convicted felon, his prints were on file for comparison. Further evidence was found when the police raided Farrant's Portsmouth apartment. They found a notepad there and were able to use a forensic method to determine what had been written on a page that had been torn out. It was a note that Farrant had apparently written to Glenda Hoskins;

"Take these instructions to be very serious. Fuck me about or refuse to do anything I ask and you will be tied up and gagged. I will not repeat myself. You will not get a second chance. If I have to use violence to get what I want, I will. It will make no difference to me, I am going to get what I want either way. The choice is yours.

"Be good and willing to me and you will come to no harm. I will be gentle, but remember you must show willing and be responsive."

The police believed that Farrant had given this note to Glenda to intimidate her into complying with his sexual demands. Then, after he'd had his way with her, he'd dragged her to the bathroom and drowned her in the tub.

But where was Farrant? Since Glenda's white Ford Escort was missing from the scene, investigators believed that Farrant had used it to escape. The vehicle would later be found abandoned on a London street, but that turned out to be a diversionary tactic by the killer. Farrant had, in fact, left the U.K., traveling by ferry from Ramsgate in Kent to Ostend in Belgium. From there, he had made his way to the south of France. He would eventually be arrested there in July 1996.

Farrant was extradited back to Britain where he was charged with the murder of Glenda Hoskins and the attempted murder of Ann Fidler. He denied the latter charge outright. As for Glenda's death, he claimed that it had been an accident. According to him, he and Glenda had had consensual sex, and Glenda had later died after accidentally falling into the bathtub, striking her head and drowning. It was never likely to be a story that a jury would believe. Even if they had been inclined to, there was considerable forensic evidence, including DNA from blood and semen, which connected Farrant to both crimes.

Victor Farrant was found guilty of murder and of attempted murder at his January 1998 trial. "This murder was so terrible and you are so dangerous that in your case, the sentence of life should mean just that," the judge said in his summation. "You should never be released."

Mixed Blessings

Officer Richard Freeman guided his police cruiser through the near-deserted streets of East Rutherford, New Jersey. It was Easter Sunday, April 7, 1996, and Freeman was getting towards the end of his shift. His last drive-by would take him through the borough's industrial precinct, a maze of offices and warehouses on the banks of the Passaic River. Given that the place was all but deserted, he expected it to be no more than a routine sweep before he headed back to the station.

But then, just as Freeman turned his cruiser onto Madison Street, he spotted something. Two cars stood in the parking lot of a company called ECI Technology. Nothing unusual in that except that the vehicles had been pulled right to the water's edge and both had their trunk lids up. As Freeman watched, a tall man emerged from between the cars, reached into one of the trunks and removed a black bag which he carried to the water's edge and then tossed in.

Officer Freeman let out a sigh, applied his foot to the gas pedal and directed his cruiser into the parking lot. It appeared his day would not pass without incident after all. He was about to issue a citation for illegal dumping. Pulling his car in behind the two vehicles, he got out, just as the dumper was returning to pick up another load. As soon as he saw the police officer, the man froze, his eyes widening in fear. It was then that Freeman noticed that he was wearing a latex glove on his right hand and that it appeared to be covered in blood. He noticed also that there were brownish spatters on his jeans. And then came the smell, that uniquely coppery aroma that any cop who has been on the job longer than a day can recognize – blood.

Freeman drew his gun, ordered the man to face the wall, and then cuffed him. He then placed the suspect into the back of his patrol car before carrying out a search of the two vehicles – a late-model Ford Taurus and a Nissan Maxima. There were eight bags, split between the two cars. The first that Freeman opened contained a set of bloody tools – a hacksaw, two axes, several knives and a scalpel; the second contained items of clothing, all of them liberally drenched in blood; the other six bags contained a human corpse, hacked into pieces.

Back at the police station in Bergen County, the suspect identified himself as Vladimir Zelenin, a 40-year-old Russian immigrant who had been in the United States for less than a year. Zelenin appeared quite happy to cooperate with the cops, chatting away excitedly in his native Russian. The problem was that none of the officers understood a word of it, and Zelenin spoke barely a word of English. He was, however, able to provide one crucial piece of information – the name of the victim. The dead man was 48-year-old Yakov Gluzman, the husband of his cousin Rita.

The names Yakov and Rita Gluzman meant nothing to the investigators, of course, but while they waited on a Russian translator, they did some probing and soon discovered that their victim was a heavy-hitter. He was a well-respected scientist who had devoted much of his life to finding a cure for cancer. He was also a millionaire. His wife, Rita, was equally accomplished. A chemical engineer by trade, she had gained a measure of celebrity as the face of the "Refusenik" movement in the Soviet Union.

This collective of Soviet Jews had shown tremendous courage in taking on the Soviet government over immigration rights for Jews who wanted to leave the country in order to freely practice their religion. Rita, articulate and beautiful, had been an apt focal point for the movement. In fact, she had garnered so much attention that the Soviets had sought to silence her by allowing her to move to the United States in 1971. That turned out to be a bad move on their part as Rita used her freedom to campaign even harder for her cause. She even gave testimony before Congress. Eventually, international pressure began to tell on the Soviets, and they were forced to loosen their immigration policies. One of the first to benefit was Rita's husband, Yakov, who had not been allowed to leave with her in 1971. After two years apart, the couple was reunited.

Their first years in the United States were, by all accounts, a happy time for the Gluzmans. Yakov was hired by Cold Spring Harbor, a renowned microbiology laboratory on Long Island. There, he worked as a senior scientist on a team headed by Dr. James D. Watson, the Nobel-prize-winning biologist who, together with Francis Crick, discovered the molecular structure of DNA. While working at the lab, Gluzman developed a technique that would become the standard for cancer researchers worldwide. While that accomplishment went wholly unnoticed by the general public, it earned Gluzman massive kudos among his fellow scientists.

In 1989, Gluzman left Cold Spring Harbor and took a $180,000-a-year job at Lederle Labs in Rockland County, New York. That upgrade in salary allowed him to buy a sprawling mansion worth half-a-million dollars, in the exclusive North Jersey community of Upper Saddle River. He and Rita also invested in a small electronics business, ECI Technologies, which Rita ran and which was successful from the outset. The Gluzmans, who had been living in Soviet deprivation just a few years earlier, now estimated their net worth at $1.3 million. It was about as patent an example of living the American Dream as you are likely to find.

But there was another cliché that fit the Gluzmans' situation equally well, the old adage that you should be careful what you wish for, because you just might get it. Success turned out to be a mixed blessing. Where the might of the Soviet empire had failed to come between Yakov and Rita, the might of the US dollar would succeed admirably.

Yakov was a modest man, at his happiest when he was leaning over a microscope, never one to concern himself with the trappings of success. Rita was different, a shopaholic who lavished thousands on luxuries and seldom passed up the opportunity to whip out her credit card. Her cosmetics bill alone could have kept a small family in house and board. That profligate spending soon proved to be an area of conflict between the couple. Another sticking point was their hilltop mansion in Upper Saddle River. Rita called it a "shack" and insisted that they move to a bigger property. Yakov's refusal to sell up only served to accentuate the growing tensions between them.

By 1994, things between Yakov and Rita had deteriorated to the point where they were constantly at each other's throats. The struggle was invariably over money. Rita wanted to spend more of it while Yakov insisted on austerity. The situation was hardly helped by their different career trajectories. Yakov's was going from strength-to-strength while Rita's was faltering. ECI Technology was barely keeping its head above water, and the reason was obvious. Every spare cent was being siphoned off by its owner for personal use.

Given the diverging paths the Gluzmans were on, it was always likely that matters would come to a head. That schism came in the fall of 1994, when Yakov told Rita that he wanted a divorce. He was planning to move to Israel, he said, in order to be close to his father. What he didn't mention to Rita was that he was in love with someone else, a young woman named Raisa Korenblit, whom he had met during one of his trips abroad.

Rita was nonetheless devastated. She may not have loved Yakov anymore, but she certainly loved the lifestyle that his money bought. She begged him to stay, and Yakov eventually agreed to give their 25-year marriage another shot. Over the next ten months, the couple cohabited under an uneasy truce, but in February 1995, Yakov informed Rita that it wasn't working. He moved out, taking a small apartment in Pearl River, New York, not far from Lederle Labs. Ten months after that, he filed for divorce, citing his wife's "mental cruelty."

By early 1996, Rita Gluzman found herself in a desperate situation. She had already burned through the $90,000 that Yakov had given her when he'd moved out a year earlier, her business continued to fail, and her divorce – bitter to begin with – had turned acrimonious. The low point came when she was caught pocketing items at a New Jersey pharmacy and charged with shoplifting. Then, in March 1996, she hit on a plan, one that could make all of her problems go away in the blink of an eye. In order to carry it out, she enlisted the help of her cousin, Vladimir Zelenin.

Zelenin owed Rita big-time. A year earlier, she had helped him leave his native Russia and had set him up with a job as a computer technician at her company. So when Rita first floated the idea of getting rid of Yakov, Zelenin barely flinched. His only concern was for his job. What would happen to ECI Technology if Yakov was gone? Do this for me and you'll never have to work again, Rita assured him. And with that, Vladimir Zelenin's full cooperation was obtained.

Rita's plan was as simple as it was brutal. She had obtained a key to Yakov's apartment and knew his schedule well. Yakov often spent his Saturday evenings at the lab, arriving home at around 11:30 p.m. That was when they would strike.

The date was set for April 6, 1994. On that pleasant spring evening, Rita and Zelenin set off for Yakov's apartment in a late-model Ford Taurus registered to ECI Technology. In the trunk was a bag containing two axes, a hacksaw, a scalpel, knives, black garbage bags and lots of household cleaning products. Arriving at around 10:30, they left their car in a shadowy spot, half-a-block away. Then they walked to the apartment and let themselves in, using Rita's key. They didn't have long to wait. Yakov Gluzman was nothing if not punctual.

It was Zelinin who struck the first blow, swinging at Yakov as he reached for the light switch in the living room. As Yakov crumbled to the floor, Rita joined the fray, falling on her estranged husband with such pent-up fury that one of her blows struck Zelenin's right hand. In no time at all, Yakov's head was reduced to a bloody mess. Then Rita took a knife and plunged it into his heart. Just to make sure, she told her cousin.

Yakov Gluzman was dead. Now came the gruesome task of hacking his body apart for disposal. Not that the bloody work seemed to bother Rita. She gave specific instructions that no part could be left big enough for identification. The fingertips needed to be cut off. So too, the nose and lips. All in all, Yakov would be carved into 65 pieces, with Zelenin doing most of the cutting, while Rita got to work cleaning up the evidence of their grisly handiwork. Then Yakov's remains were stuffed into nine black plastic garbage bags, some of which were loaded into the Taurus, some of which ended up in the trunk of Yakov's Nissan Maxima.

Now the murder plot moved into its next phase. According to the plan, they would drive the 30 miles to ECI Technology's East Rutherford office in the two cars, Zelenin in the Taurus, Rita in the Maxima. Zelenin would then drive Rita home in the Nissan, leaving the Taurus at ECI. After dropping Rita off, he would return to East Rutherford, dump Yakov's remains in the Passaic River and then get rid of the Maxima.

All of this was to happen before sunrise, but Rita had underestimated the amount of time the dismemberment and clean-up would take. By the time they dropped the Taurus off at ECI, the sky was already graying; by the time Rita finally reached her Upper Saddle River home, the sun was out. Zelenin then drove back to ECI Technology to start dropping bags in the river. He had made only one drop when he was spotted by Officer Freeman.

If there is one thing that could be said about Rita Gluzman, it is that she was a survivor. Not only had she survived her confrontation with the Soviet state, but she had also negotiated her way through a fractious marriage and come out on top. Now that survival instinct kicked in again. By the time Bergen County officials arrived to arrest her, Rita was gone. So, too, was her passport.

The police immediately sent out an urgent alert to all nearby airports, but those came up empty because Rita had no intention of hopping a flight – at least not yet. Her plan was to lay low until the heat was off, and to that extent, she drove east, towards Long Island, stealing a set of New York plates en route. In Cold Spring Harbor, where she and Yakov had once lived, she broke into an unoccupied bungalow and hunkered down to consider her next move. She remained there until Friday, April 12, when she was surprised by a maid doing her routine cleaning rounds. Rita tried to flee but was apprehended by security guards who in turn called the police.

Rita Gluzman was booked on burglary and trespassing in Nassau County, Long Island. In the meantime, Vladimir Zelenin had been charged with second-degree murder and had spilled the beans about Yakov's death, implicating Rita. But the case against the murderous wife was not as clear cut as it appeared. With no forensics linking her to the crime scene, it was essentially her word against Zenelin's. Who was a jury likely to believe? The wife of a respected scientist or a recent Russian émigré? The case looked to be slipping away and matters became even more urgent when Rita was granted bail.

At this stage, Rita Gluzman's attorney was confident that the state would not risk bringing murder charges against her. He confidently advised her that the worst they could do was accessory to murder. But he had forgotten about the recently enacted Domestic Violence Statute. This law gives jurisdiction to the federal government when a person crosses state lines to commit an act of domestic violence. At that point, it had only been used in a few cases, always to indict male offenders. Rita Gluzman would be the first woman to face prosecution under the statute.

Gluzman appeared in federal court during April 1997, a little more than a year after the murder of her husband. She entered a not guilty plea and vehemently denied on the stand that she had played any part in Yakov's death. But Vladimir Zelenin's testimony was compelling, and the jury chose to believe him rather than her. Found guilty of the charges against her, Gluzman was sentenced to life in prison without parole.

The Horrible Death of Red-Hot Carla

On the afternoon of Tuesday, October 14, 2009, a police officer in the Belgian city of Liège received a call from an anxious-sounding woman. She said that she was worried about her neighbor, who she hadn't seen in the last 24 hours. Barely able to stifle a yawn, the officer took down the details, noting that the "missing" woman was neither elderly nor frail. He then told the caller not to concern herself and hung up. He had no intention of taking the matter further.

The caller, however, wasn't ready to give up. Deep into the night, she called again, this time getting a different officer but a similar response. As the officer curtly informed her, the police did not have the resources to go looking for every adult who dropped out of sight for a day or two.

The following afternoon, the Liège police received a call of a more serious nature – a gunshot had been heard in a residential neighborhood. The address was familiar to them. It was the same one mentioned in the missing person reports. Half suspecting that the caller had made up the gunshot to force them into checking on her neighbor, a couple of officers set off for the middle-class suburb of Vottem, about three miles from the city center. There, the address they'd been given led them to a two-story, red-brick terrace, identical to every other residence on the street. The front door was locked and no amount of leaning on the bell brought any response. The officers then tried peering through the front window but found their view obscured by a heavy lace curtain. They then decided to force the lock.

The smell of death is a familiar one to all but the greenest of rookie cops. The officers had just entered the hallway when they picked it up. The slightly metallic smell of blood, a faint whiff of cordite and, overlaying it all, the sickly-sweet stench of decaying flesh. That latter smell wasn't coming from the man slumped across the couch in the front room. He was a relatively fresh kill, the blood on his face still a fading shade of crimson. The facial wound, and the gun clutched limply in his right hand, suggested suicide. This was probably the gunshot that the neighbor had heard. More out of procedure than expectation, one of the officers went over and placed his fingers against the man's throat. Incredibly, he felt a faint pulse. "Call an ambulance," he shouted to his partner.

"What?"

"Call a goddamn ambulance. He's still alive!"

That exhortation sent the other cop scrambling back to the patrol car. Soon the ambulance had arrived, and the gunshot victim was being raced to the hospital where doctors confirmed that he was indeed alive – alive but in a coma with a poor prognosis for recovery.

While all of that was going on, police officers were continuing their search of the townhouse. And their sense of smell had not betrayed them. There was a second victim in the house, this one most definitely dead, and for several days by the look of it. She was a young woman, lying face up on a bed in an upstairs bedroom. But perhaps "face up" is a poor choice of words. Her facial features had been all but obliterated.

Neighbors soon filled detectives in on the identity of the victims. He was Stéphane Fontaine, 43 years old, and described by more than one respondent as a "lay about." She was Carla Sainclair and was described as an actress. What the neighbors failed to mention, but what the police soon discovered, was that Carla's "acting" was of the adult variety. She was the star of porn movies as well as x-rated websites where she was billed as Red-Hot Carla.

But who had killed her? So far the police were working on two possible theories. Either Fontaine had committed the murder and then tried to kill himself; or some third party had shot both Carla and Fontaine and tried to make it look like a murder/suicide. With Fontaine unable to answer questions, investigators started delving into the backgrounds of the couple for answers.

What they found out about "Red-Hot" Carla Sainclair was surprising. For starters, she was from a stable upper-middle-class family and had been an excellent student who had harbored dreams of becoming a journalist. Her real name was Anne Derouck, and she'd once worked as a sales assistant at an upmarket department store. But then she had discovered the murky world of "gentlemen's clubs" and had started stripping to make extra cash. Anne was a pretty, dark-haired girl with a curvaceous body, and she was popular with punters. It was only a short hop from there to prostitution.

But Anne wasn't just in this for the money. As she freely admitted to other working girls, she couldn't get enough of sex. So much so that she started going to "swinging parties." It was at one of those parties, in 2000, that she met Stèphane Fontaine.

Anne and Stèphane made an unlikely pairing. She was 20 years old, verging on beautiful, and with an air of innocence about her, despite her profession. He was 14 years her senior, stoutly built and with close-cropped hair that gave him a thuggish appearance. And looks, in this case, were not deceiving. Stèphane Fontaine was a hardened criminal who had spent time in prison for bank robbery and kidnapping. At the time he met Anne, he had just been released from his latest period of incarceration and was working at a biscuit factory.

It is easy to see what attracted Stèphane to Anne, not quite so simple to understand her preoccupation with him. Yet, soon after their first encounter, she was describing him to friends as her "one and only love." She'd also allowed him to move into her apartment where he became a kept man or, more aptly, her pimp.

It was Fontaine who came up with the idea of rebranding Anne Derouck as Carla Sainclair (after the well-known French porn star, Laure Sainclair), and it was he who encouraged her to expand her horizons. Soon Carla was traveling throughout Europe to participate in sex parties and had set up her website, complete with webcam, where she would strip and perform sex acts at $500 a time. The couple had by now moved into the house in Vottem, where one bedroom was set aside for Carla to entertain her clients. Then, in 2008, she auditioned for a role in a porn movie and was hired on the spot and given a long-term contact. Over the next year-and-a-half, she would star in seven adult movies and also appear in countless clips intended for online consumption.

Carla's career was booming, and Fontaine, more than anyone else, was the beneficiary. She now had a profile within the adult industry and no longer needed him as a "promoter." That left Fontaine free to loaf around the house, and he spent most of that time getting drunk and popping pills. In early 2009, Carla began complaining to friends that Fontaine was becoming increasingly violent towards her. She hinted that she was thinking of leaving him but said that she still loved him and couldn't "just walk away."

On Friday, October 9, 2009, Carla attended a sex fair in the town of Tournai, some 100 miles away, where she was the star attraction. She arrived home to find a drunk and broody Stèphane. An argument soon flared, lubricated by the wine both of them were consuming. When it eventually subsided, Carla sat down to write a note. It would prove a tragic harbinger of what was to come.

'I, Anne Derouck, testify that Stéphane Fontaine has threatened to kill me. He threatens me openly. If I am to die, I want an autopsy to be carried out on my body. I declare that I do not want to die. I am sorry to say it but if I am to die, the guilty one will be Stéphane Fontaine.'

That note was recovered during a search of the Vottem house and pointed investigators in the direction of the first scenario they had considered, the murder/suicide. The nature of Carla's injuries certainly pointed to a personal motive. This crime had been committed by someone who bore great animosity towards her. She had been shot four times in the head at close range, the bullets penetrating her temple, forehead, and right eye. The lack of other injuries on the body suggested that she was probably shot while she slept, and her blood/alcohol level suggested that she may have been passed out. According to the pathologist, she had been dead for three days by the time Fontaine decided to take his own life.

That Fontaine had failed in that attempt was not down to a lack of trying. Doctors considered it a minor miracle that he had survived. The gun barrel had been placed in his mouth and the bullet had penetrated his palate on an upward trajectory. It had entered the left lobe of his brain, destroying the optic nerve of his left eye. It had rendered him comatose and, according to experts, it was a coma from which he might never emerge.

Fontaine, however, proved to be far more resilient than the medical experts gave him credit for. On January 10, 2010, three months after the murder, he walked from the hospital in handcuffs, flanked by two burly constables. He was taken to the hospital at Lantin Prison, where he tried to answer police questions.

But Fontaine's memory was predictably sketchy. He could remember arguing with Carla over his refusal to go with her to the sex fair in Tournai, but he could recall little else. Specifically, the three days from Carla's murder to his own suicide attempt were a blank. The police would have to rely on neighbors to fill in the gaps. They reported seeing him standing at the upstairs window for hours at a time, as though staring into a void. What the neighbors didn't know was that Carla was just feet away, lying on the bed with her face, and her life, destroyed.

Whether or not Fontaine's memory lapse was the real thing or a cynical attempt to evade justice, we shall never know. In any case, it did not save him. Found guilty of murder in March 2012, he was sentenced to 25 years in prison. And perhaps that was not the worst of his punishment. The self-inflicted gunshot wound had left him disfigured and totally blind in his left eye. He will also be mentally impaired for the rest of his days.

Pour Some Sugar

The story of Henrietta Robinson is one of the most curious in the annals of American crime. Henrietta was a beautiful but troubled young woman who lived in Troy, New York, in the mid-1800s. She was known to carry a pistol and to produce it at the slightest sign of trouble, whether real or imagined. In fact, it often *was* imagined since Henrietta suffered from a condition that we would today recognize as paranoid schizophrenia.

Henrietta's particular brand of madness was well known to her neighbors. More than once, they were surprised to receive a visit from the police, responding to a complaint of persecution laid by Henrietta. As the perplexed neighbors explained on these occasions, they barely exchanged the time of day with the woman. Henrietta was also fond of wandering the streets at night, wearing only a nightdress but packing her trusty pistol on her hip. Anyone who dared ask what she was doing would find that same pistol shoved in his face, challenged to give Henrietta a reason to use it. Quite often, acquaintances of hers would find her on their doorstep in the early morning hours, asking to borrow a dress.

Henrietta would invariably explain that she'd set off on some
chore, only to realize halfway through it that she wasn't
appropriately attired.

And it wasn't only Henrietta's odd behavior that had tongues
wagging in Troy. Another popular pastime was to speculate about
her identity and background. Much of this conjecture was initiated
by Henrietta herself, or rather by the tall tales she liked to tell. She
hinted that Henrietta Robinson was not her real name and
variously claimed to be the daughter of a lord; the offspring of a
humble Irish fisherman from Vermont; and a fugitive from corrupt
justice in "the old country." One thing was consistent, though; in all
of the stories she told, Henrietta was always the victim, the target
of some or other conspiracy.

In 1853, Henrietta Robinson was living in a cottage in Troy, with a
servant girl and an elderly gardener. Across from her home stood
Lanagan's General Store, run by Timothy Lanagan and his family.
The Lanagans lived in an apartment above the store, and they also
owned the tavern next door, a popular spot with the locals for
drinking and dancing. Henrietta did not participate in these
festivities, but she did sometimes send her gardener to the store to
buy beer or, on occasion, brandy. In fact, her orders became so
frequent that neighbors speculated that she must be permanently
inebriated. Perhaps that was the cause of her peculiar behavior.

One day, sometime in 1852, Henrietta showed up at Lanagan's
Tavern and joined the rowdies at the bar, matching them drink for
drink. Thereafter, she became a regular at the bar and also a
constant thorn in Timothy Lanagan's side. On more than one

occasion, she was forcibly ejected from the building after she drew her pistol and threatened to shoot one of the patrons. And yet, she always made her peace with Lanagan and was allowed back while carrying her firearm.

Which brings us to the morning of May 25, 1853. The day had started in typical fashion for Henrietta. Around mid-morning, she'd sent her gardener to buy a quart of beer, but she'd soon polished that off and had then headed across the street to Lanagan's. There, true to form, she'd gotten into an argument with one of the patrons and had drawn her pistol. Mrs. Lanagan then entered the fray and asked Henrietta to leave.

At around one o'clock that afternoon, Henrietta knocked on the door of the Lanagans' apartment and told Mrs. Lanagan that she wanted to apologize for her earlier behavior. Mrs. Lanagan appeared happy to accept the apology. In fact, she'd just sat down to lunch with her husband and her sister-in-law, Catherine Lubee, who was visiting. She asked Henrietta to join them, and Henrietta was happy to accept.

Henrietta, although obviously tipsy, was the picture of propriety during the meal. Afterwards, she suggested repaying the Lanagan's hospitality by treating them to some beer on her account. Mrs. Lanagan politely declined, but her husband and Miss Lubee accepted the offer. Lanagan then went down to the store to fetch the beer, while Henrietta asked Mrs. Lanagan for some sugar. She always put it in her beer, she explained, to temper the bitterness.

By now, Lanagan was back, and soon the beer mugs had been filled. However, he hadn't brought enough to go around, and he soon returned to the store to fetch another quart bottle. When he returned, he noticed that Henrietta had added sugar to his glass and also to the glass of Miss Lubee. This wasn't how he usually took his tipple, but it would have been impolite to complain, and so he filled the glasses and then proposed a toast to their guest.

But Henrietta appeared to have lost a taste for the ale. She took only a cursory sip and then announced suddenly that she had to leave. Accustomed to her eccentricities, the Lanagans attached no significance to her sudden departure. Mr. Lanagan and Miss Lubee drained their glasses and then split Henrietta's glass between them. Within hours, both had come down with severe stomach cramps, diarrhea, and vomiting. A doctor was called and diagnosed arsenic poisoning.

There could be little doubt as to who was responsible. Mrs. Lanagan told the police about the beer Henrietta had bought for her hosts and the "sugar" she'd added to it; a local druggist was found who had recently sold some arsenic to Henrietta; and arsenic was found in Henrietta's cottage. Henrietta was soon under arrest, with the charge upgraded to murder when both Mr. Lanagan and Miss Lubee died over the next few days.

Criminal trials were usually swiftly conducted in those days, but in Henrietta's case, there were several delays, meaning that she was not officially indicted until February 1854, nine months after the murders. Her trial did not commence until May, and in the interim, she tried to commit suicide by taking vitriol. How the poison made its way into the prison was never fully explained. In any case, the dose that Henrietta had swallowed was not enough to cause death, only severe pain and considerable discomfort.

With the story now commanding headlines throughout the United States and Canada, a new chapter was added to Henrietta's legend. It appeared that Henrietta Robinson was not her real name, and various stories emerged, each claiming that it had uncovered her true identity. According to one story, she was Mrs. Campbell, a drinking house proprietress from the suburbs of Quebec; according to another, she was the daughter of a Montreal medical doctor, who'd died nine years earlier in a lunatic asylum; another held that her father was a landed Irish gentleman, who had disinherited her after she'd eloped with the son of his steward. One of the stories even resulted in a lawsuit as William F. Wood sued the Troy Times for printing a story in which the newspaper claimed that Henrietta was Mr. Wood's estranged daughter.

Whatever her true identity, it was under the name Henrietta Robinson that she appeared in court on May 22, 1854, charged with two counts of murder. With little chance of pleading innocence to the crimes, her defense opted on an insanity defense, citing Henrietta's history of erratic behavior and her complete lack of motive in the double homicide. The prosecution countered that Henrietta's erratic behavior was due to her state of perpetual inebriation and that the motive was vengefulness. She'd been thrown out of Lanagan's bar so many times that her ejection on the morning of May 25, 1853, proved to be the final straw. As always with Henrietta, she did not look to her own behavior, but instead believed that the Lanagans were persecuting her for no good reason.

This was the version of events that the jury decided to accept. They decided that, in spite of her antics, Henrietta was not insane and was therefore responsible for her actions. Upon hearing the verdict of guilty to two counts of first-degree murder, Henrietta was immediately on her feet. "Shame on you, judge!" she shouted. "Shame on you! There is corruption here! There is corruption in the court!" One would have expected no less of a response from paranoid Henrietta.

The sentence was, of course, taken on appeal which delayed matters for another year. Ultimately, though, the defense attorney's motion for a new trial was denied, and on June 14, 1855, Henrietta Robinson was sentenced to hang, with the date of her execution set for August 3. That sanction was never carried out, though, since the governor of New York decided to commute the sentence to life in prison. Henrietta was not pleased on hearing the outcome. She complained that she had made peace with God and had been ready to die.

Henrietta Robinson would spend eighteen years at Sing Sing before being relocated to a facility in Auburn, New York. In 1890, she was transferred to the Mateawan Hospital for the Criminally Insane where she spent the last fifteen years of her life. She died in 1905, at the age of 78, having never revealed her true identity or the reason why she had decided to murder two innocent people, one of whom was a complete stranger to her.

A Good Day to Die

Clarence Ray Allen

The story reads like something out of a bad crime novel – a wannabee mob boss; a crew of bumbling accomplices; a series of bungled small-time crimes escalating to murder; a final gun battle worthy of a Quentin Tarantino movie. Yet every piece of the Clarence Ray Allen story is true. Allen was a Native American of the Choctaw tribe, born dirt poor in Blair, Oklahoma, in 1930. Growing up, he received very little education and was in the fields picking cotton almost as soon as he could walk. Had he continued on that path, he'd have spent his life at back-breaking labor and would more than likely have ended up drinking himself into an early grave.

But Ray Allen was a determined man and, despite his lack of schooling, an intelligent one. In the early '50s, he moved to Fresno, California, where he worked for a time as a farm laborer before setting up a security company. Ray had never been shy of hard work, and he was a charismatic man, blessed with "the gift of the gab." His business flourished and, in the years that followed, made him a millionaire. He'd arrived in Fresno with the clothes on his back. He ended up owning a sprawling horse ranch and a private airplane.

Most men would have looked back on these achievements with a sense of pride and accomplishment. Not Ray Allen. There had always been a dark side to his character, an egotistical drive that veered him towards criminality. There had been rumors for years that he was using his company as a front for illicit activities and that he may even have robbed some of the properties he had been hired to protect. Ray, of course, denied these allegations, and there was never any evidence to prove them.

But perhaps the stories about his criminal activities gave Ray an idea because, by the late sixties, the Allen ranch had become a magnet for delinquents and ne'er-do-goods. These young men could usually be found hanging out by the pool, listening to Ray's stories and hanging on every word that he spoke. Eventually, Ray had the idea of putting their dubious talents to work. He formed them into a criminal crew which he labelled, with a narcissistic lack of originality, the Ray Allen Gang.

The Allen Gang's activities were mostly burglaries of residential and business premises. But Ray lorded it over his subordinates like some Native American Al Capone. His orders were to be obeyed without question, as were all of his rules. The most important of these was no snitching. "Snitches sleep with the fishes," he informed his young accomplices. To prove his point, he showed them a newspaper article about two people who had been found shot to death in Nevada. Although he didn't specifically say so, he hinted that he'd had something to do with it.

Despite the small-time nature of most of the gang's activities, they were prolific enough to make Ray Allen a handsome little side income. Ray wasn't usually involved in the break-ins himself. He was the planner, and he was good at it, using his security contacts to gain intel on the properties he aimed to rob. It all went well until 1974, when he made the mistake of targeting Fran's Market, a Fresno business owned by his friend, Raymond Schletewitz.

Ray's plan for the robbery went something like this. He would get his son, Roger, to invite Bryon Schletewitz (Raymond's son) to the ranch for a swim. While Bryon was in the pool, Ray would go through his pockets and steal the keys to the store. Roger's girlfriend, Mary Sue Kitts, would meanwhile cozy up to Bryon, getting him to take her out on a date. That would give the gang the opportunity to rob Fran's. They'd enter using the key, open the safe, and empty it of cash. It seemed almost too easy.

And it was. While Bryon was out wining and dining Mary Sue the following night, Ray, Roger, and gang members Carl Mayfield and Lee Furrow entered the market. The safe was easy to locate but difficult to open, and so the men simply carried it out to their truck and drove with it back to the ranch. There, they found that it contained the paltry sum of $500 in cash. There was, however, $10,000 in money orders. Soon those vouchers were being cashed all over Southern California.

The robbery had gone more smoothly than any of them could have expected. No one had been hurt and, more importantly, no one

suspected Ray Allen. But then Mary Sue Kitts had an attack of
conscience and confessed to Bryon Schletewitz that she had duped
him. Bryon, in turn, confronted Roger Allen and demanded to
know if what Mary Sue had told him was true. Roger admitted it
was, and Bryon then took the story to his parents.

Before the Schletewitzs could go to the police, though, Ray arrived
at their house running damage control. He swore that he'd had
nothing to do with the robbery, although he admitted that he knew
who was behind it. Then he issued a warning to the family, saying
that the perpetrators were going to burn their house down if they
reported the robbery. To give more credence to his statement, he
sent gang member Lee Furrow to do a drive-by shooting of their
home that night. The matter went no further.

But now Ray had some housekeeping to take care of. He'd always
warned that snitches would be killed, and Mary Sue Kitts had shot
her mouth off. She would have to be dealt with. He instructed Lee
Furrow to invite Mary Sue to a party which would be held at the
apartment of Shirley Doeckel, Ray's girlfriend. There Furrow
would ask if she wanted to get high and would offer her a pill.
Except that the pill would actually contain cyanide, and Mary Sue
would soon be dead. The gang would then dispose of her body.

At first, Furrow balked at the idea. He said that Mary Sue was just a
kid. She was only 17 years old, but at just over 5 feet and weighing
100 pounds, she looked much younger. Ray was adamant, though.
Mary Sue had to die. He also reminded Furrow of the gang's other
rule – all of Ray's orders were to be obeyed without question.

Eventually, Furrow agreed to go through with it. Mary Sue was lured to the party and offered the pill. When she refused it, a bewildered Furrow phoned Ray, asking what he should do. Ray angrily told him to use his initiative and hung up the phone. A series of near-comedic calls then passed between the would-be assassin and his boss. Finally, Ray said that he would come over and do the job himself, adding that if he had to do that, he'd be committing two murders, not one. That stirred Furrow into action. After Mary Sue again declined his offer of the pill, he strangled her to death. Her body was later dismembered and dropped into the Friant-Kern canal. It has never been found.

After the murder of Mary Sue Kitts, the Allen gang laid low for a while. Ray secretly sent Lee Furrow out of town, although he hinted that he'd had Lee killed for his reluctance to carry out orders. At around that time, Ray recruited two new members, Allen Robinson and Benjamin Meyer, giving them the usual pep talk about how snitches were dealt with in his organization. "We had a broad helping us who got mouthy so we had to waste her," he boasted. "She's now sleeping with the fishes."

Six months after the Kitts murder, the Allen gang got back to business. Ray had developed a "foolproof" plan for robbing K-Mart stores, and on February 10, 1977, he put it to the test at the K-Mart in Tulare, California. It went without a hitch, netting the gang $16,000. However, Ray was unhappy with the performance of Allen Robinson during the robbery. He considered killing Robinson but, in the end, banished him, warning him to leave town.

Robinson was replaced in the gang by Larry Green. But during the next robbery, at the Visalia K-Mart in March 1977, Green, really screwed up. While holding his gun to the head of a K-Mart employee, he spotted a movement behind him, turned and fired, hitting a customer. The gang then fled, reaching the parking lot just as the police arrived with sirens blaring. Green, Ben Meyer and Ray Allen were arrested at the scene.

Clarence Ray Allen was tried and convicted of robbery, attempted robbery and assault with a deadly weapon. But there was worse to come for the gang boss. Once in custody, his cohorts quickly abandoned their "no snitching" oath. They all started talking. As a result, Allen and Lee Furrow were charged with the first-degree murder of Mary Sue Kitts. Furrow subsequently struck a deal and agreed to testify against his boss. At the trial, there was also testimony from Bryon Schletewitz, Carl Mayfield, Shirley Doeckel, and Ben Meyer. Allen never stood a chance. He was sentenced to life in prison without parole.

Allen was sent to serve his time at the State Prison in Folsom, California. But if his former gang members thought that they were free of him, they were sorely mistaken. Stung by their betrayal, Ray was soon plotting his revenge, recruiting fellow inmate Billy Ray Hamilton to his cause. Hamilton was due to be paroled soon. He was offered $25,000 to "take care of some people," and quickly agreed. Ray then handed him a slip of paper with the names of the gang members who had betrayed him. Top of the list, though, were Bryon Schletewitz and his parents.

If Ray Allen had one flaw in his make-up as a wannabe mob boss, it was his inability to hire reliable help. In Billy Ray Hamilton, he had recruited another loose cannon. Shortly after his release from Folsom, Hamilton met with Ray's son, Kenny, who provided him with a sawed-off shotgun, a .32 caliber revolver, and ammunition. That same night, Hamilton visited Fran's Market in the company of an accomplice, his girlfriend, Connie Barbo. The plan was to catch the owners just before closing time when the store was likely to be empty. On this evening, however, there was a 15-year old Mexican boy in the store, and so the couple bailed. They returned 24 hours later, and this time, there were no pangs of conscience to deflect them from their mission.

Hamilton entered the market first, waving the shotgun around wildly and telling everyone to lie on the ground. Including Bryon Schletewitz, there were four employees in the store at the time. Hamilton rounded them all up and then marched Bryon to the stockroom while Barbo held the other employees at bay with the revolver. Moments later, there was a loud boom. Then Hamilton returned and demanded to know where the safe was. When employee Douglas White told him that there was no safe, Hamilton shot him in the chest, killing him instantly. Another employee, Josephine Rocha, started sobbing hysterically, whereupon Hamilton shot her, too. He then turned the gun on the last survivor, Joe Rios, shooting him in the face. Miraculously, Rios would survive.

But, as far as Hamilton knew, he'd killed everyone. He and Barbo therefore turned and ran, hoping to make their escape before the cops arrived. They'd just exited the store, however, when a loud voice ordered them to stop. Hamilton was momentarily surprised.

He hadn't heard any sirens. But then he spotted him, not a cop but a civilian, standing off to the side with a handgun raised. Jack Abbott lived near the market and had come to investigate after hearing shots fired.

Hamilton wasn't about to be taken by some would-be hero. He raised the shotgun and fired at Abbott, who shot back. A fierce gunfight ensued during which Barbo ran back into the store and hid in the Ladies Room. Then Abbott was hit, allowing Hamilton to make a dash for his getaway vehicle. He was hit in the foot as he fled, but still managed to scramble into the car and race off. Seconds later, the sound of sirens could be heard in the distance.

The Fresno police walked in on a bloodbath. Bryon Schletewitz, Doug White, and Josephine Rocha were dead. Joe Rios and Jack Abbott were injured, Rios seriously so. He was rushed to hospital by ambulance. In the meanwhile, officers conducted a search of the building and found Connie Barbo cowering in a bathroom stall. Taken into custody, she soon gave up the name of Billy Ray Hamilton. He, in the meantime, was making his way north to the home of a criminal associate in Modesto. While hiding out there, he made the ill-advised decision to rob a liquor store and was arrested.

Hamilton, to his credit, did not rat out Ray Allen. It was Ray's own son who did the deed. Arrested on drugs charges, Kenny offered to testify against his father. In return, he wanted to be placed in protective custody. His father, he said, could reach him anywhere.

Clarence Ray Allen went on trial in June 1981, charged with three counts of murder and three counts of conspiracy to commit murder. Taking the stand in his own defense, Allen denied all of the charges against him, except helping to dispose of Mary Sue Kitts's body. He denied, however, that he'd had anything to do with her death. He insisted that he was a robber, not a killer, and spoke with obvious pride when describing the planning that had gone into the K-Mart heists. Even on trial for his life, Ray Allen could not resist playing the criminal mastermind.

In the end, Ray's renowned powers of persuasion were not good enough to convince the jury. He was found guilty of all charges and sentenced to die. A subsequent appeal, citing his advanced years and physical infirmities, was denied.

Clarence Ray Allen was put to death by lethal injection on January 17, 2006. At age 76, he became the oldest person ever executed by the State of California. Celebrating his Native American heritage, Allen went to his death with an eagle feather laid on his chest, a medicine bag around his neck, and a beaded headband encircling his head. His last words were: "It's a good day to die. I love you all. Goodbye."

Murder in the Playroom

Rahan Arshad

As any fan of the TV reality show *Married at First Sight* will tell you, tying the knot with someone you've never met before is not without its challenges. Not even the intervention of "scientific matching" and guidance from a panel of "relationship experts" guarantees a successful outcome. In fact, the odds of such relationships succeeding are 50/50 at best, no more than blind luck. And yet, in some cultures, arranged marriages are a long-standing tradition. Such unions are not love matches between individuals, but rather arrangements agreed between families. The betrothed most often see each other for the first time on their wedding day. Love, compatibility, and all of that, can come later.

Thus it was with Rahan Arshad and his bride, Uzma. The pair were first cousins, brought together by their parents. And at first it seemed like a good match, one that produced three children, Adam, Abbas, and Henna, in 11 years. Rahan, according to friends and neighbors, was deeply in love with his wife and devoted to his children. He was a hard worker who put in long shifts as a taxi driver in Manchester, England. Uzma, meanwhile, worked in the canteen of a local school. Their joint endeavors enabled them to buy an attractive home in Burnage. To all the world, they seemed a happy, contented family.

But behind the scenes, trouble was brewing. Rahan resented the fact that his wife so readily embraced Western culture and particularly hated her style of dress, which often consisted of tight jeans and a tee shirt. "It's not right for someone from Pakistan to dress in that way," he complained to a friend. "Especially the mother of three children."

And that wasn't the only complaint that Rahan had about Uzma. He frequently voiced the opinion that she was bad-tempered and materialistic, that she looked down on him, and spent money they couldn't afford. He even claimed that while he was always even-tempered and patient with his wife, she had once physically attacked him. It was a description that people who knew Uzma would later find difficult to square with the pleasant, smiling woman they'd come to know.

So what is it that might have caused Rahan to bad-mouth his wife in this way? It might well be that he was frustrated by his inability to exert control over her. Uzma was certainly strong-willed. She had not turned out to be the typically submissive Pakistani wife that Rahan had hoped for. A jealous and possessive man, he expected her to abide by his rules. With Uzma, that was never likely to happen.

And then there was the affair. It began when Uzma started
operating a small, home-based beautician business. That required
her to travel to the houses of her clients, and that meant that she
needed a babysitter to look after her youngest child, Henna, for a
couple of hours each day. A neighbor, Musarat Iqbal was engaged
to take on babysitting duties and, shortly after, Rahan became
convinced that his wife was sleeping with Musarat's husband,
Nikki. She would receive cellphone calls at odd hours and would
always respond in the same way. "I can't speak right now; I'm with
my husband." When Rahan asked her about the calls, she always
insisted that they were from her clients. Unconvinced, Rahan got
hold of her phone one day and scrolled through the messages.
Several were from Nikki and seemed to confirm the affair. And yet,
Uzma continued to deny that anything was going on. It served only
to fuel the growing rage inside Rahan.

The culture in which Rahan Arshad had been raised is fervently
patriarchal. Males dominate just about every aspect of society, and
women are most often cast in the traditional roles of wife and
mother. Honor plays a big part, and honor killings of children or
spouses are not unknown. Just about the greatest dishonor a
woman can pay her husband is to cheat on him.

Yet Rahan was torn. He wanted desperately to believe Uzma's
denials, even as he wanted to strike out, to gain revenge for his
bruised ego. His chance came in February 2004 when Uzma's
father died and she traveled to Pakistan to be with her family
during their period of mourning. No sooner had Uzma boarded her
flight for Lahore than Rahan visited a local realtor and put their
Burnage Lane property on the market, offering it at a knockdown

price for a quick sale. Uzma had always loved that house, and now he was going to take it away from her.

Rahan didn't stop there, though. After pocketing £90,000 from the house sale, he flew out to Pakistan with his children, dumped them with Uzma, and served her with false divorce papers. He then went on an extended holiday, leaving his wife and kids to return to the UK penniless and with nowhere to live. They ended up in a shelter for a time before securing a house through the local council. By then, Rahan was back in Britain, missing his family and regretting his impetuous actions. In desperation, he approached Rahat Ali, Uzma's oldest brother and now head of the family, and asked if he would facilitate a reconciliation. Ali agreed to do so but was none too certain that Uzma would listen.

In the end, though, Ali prevailed upon his sister to reconcile with her husband, even if it was just for the sake of the children. Whatever his other failings might be, Rahan had always been a good father. One of the conditions of the reunion was that Rahan would have to provide a home for his family, and he did so right away, purchasing a property in Cheadle Hulme, Stockport, part of Greater Manchester. He even put the property in both his and Uzma's names as a show of good faith.

But still Uzma was unconvinced. She remained in her council house for several weeks after the supposed reconciliation. Even when she eventually moved into the Cheadle Hulme property, she kept the council house as a backup, just in case things didn't work out. This would later turn out to be a major bone of contention between the couple, but for now Rahan appeared to be determined to patch things up. Where he'd previously accused his wife of being materialistic, he now embarked on a spending spree himself, buying a £30,000 BMW 320 for Uzma, toys and computers for the kids, clothes and jewelry for all of them. He also spent a small fortune decorating the new family home to his wife's taste. Uzma, though, was still suspicious of his motives. "Count the days, till he kills me," she told a friend. Sadly, that offhand comment would turn out to be predictive.

After the fact, it is easy to look back at signposts along the road to murder and identify the point at which things started to go wrong. In the case of Rahan and Uzma Arshad, it was the council house that Uzma had kept as a fallback in the event of her marriage breaking down for a second time. Once Rahan found out about it, he became incensed, convinced that Uzma was using the property for illicit liaisons with her lover, Nikki. Whether this is true or not is irrelevant. The fact is that Rahan believed it, and it filled him with righteous indignation. He had done everything to put things right with Uzma, had bought her a house, a car, forgiven her earlier transgressions. And this was how she repaid him? Before long, his mind had turned again towards revenge. Except, this time, there would be no turning back.

During July 2006, Rahan Arshad informed his family that he would shortly be taking them on a holiday to Dubai. The older children were understandably excited about this, and soon all of the neighbors had heard about the upcoming vacation. In mid-July, Rahan walked into a travel agent's office in Manchester and booked a flight, not for his family, but for himself. The destination was Bangkok, Thailand. That same day, he visited a sporting goods store and purchased a baseball bat.

And so to the night of July 28. Rahan had worked a late shift that night and returned home after his family had all retired to bed. Entering the silent house, he walked directly to the lounge where he'd stashed his recently acquired baseball bat in a corner. Picking it up, he hefted it in his hand, appreciating the weight. Then he started climbing the stairs to the master bedroom. Uzma was shaken rudely awake and found her husband standing over her, the bat in his hand. She had barely had time to register what was happening when the first blow landed. Twenty-two more blows would be rained down upon Uzma, pulping her skull and fracturing the arm she threw up in a vain effort to protect herself. She never stood a chance.

Had Rahan stopped there, had he called the police and handed himself over, there are some who might even have sympathized with him – the betrayed husband, driven to a brutal act against the woman he loved, by emotions way beyond his control. But Rahan didn't stop there. What he did next went beyond savagery. The children were woken one by one, marched down to their playroom, and there subjected to the same fate as their mother. Adam, the oldest, was only 11 years old on the night that his father bludgeoned him to death; the youngest, Henna, was just six.

Having murdered his family, Rahan now put the rest of his plan into action. He drove his wife's BMW to Manchester airport, abandoning it there, and then boarding a flight for Bangkok. Since friends and neighbors believed that the family had left for a vacation in Dubai, no concerns were raised until a month later. On August 20, 2006, police broke into the Cheadle Hulme property and discovered four corpses, so badly decomposed that they could only be identified using dental records.

Rahan, meanwhile, was living it up in Thailand. He probably thought that he had escaped British justice, but he had made a poor job of covering his tracks and was soon arrested on an international fugitive warrant and returned to the UK. On landing at Heathrow, Rahan apparently told the arresting officers, "I confess to the murder. My beautiful kids, I don't regret killing that bitch, but my kids, killing my kids..."

By the time the matter came to trial, however, Rahan was spinning a different story. He now claimed that he'd arrived home from work on the night of July 28 to find that Uzma had bludgeoned their three children to death. He'd then wrenched the baseball bat from her grasp and used it to kill her. It had been an act of revenge, he said, for the murders of his children.

Unfortunately for Rahan, that story did not gel with the known facts. If the murder had really been committed on the spur of the moment, in a fit of rage, how was it that he'd had the foresight to purchase a plane ticket to Thailand two weeks before the event? How was it that he'd bought the murder weapon that same day? In the end, it was his poorly conceived escape plan, as much as anything, that pointed to his guilt.

"You beat your wife to death in her bedroom and then coldly and deliberately you brought your sleepy children downstairs to meet their deaths," Justice Clarke said in his summation. "It was a brutal and horrific crime." He then sentenced Rahad to life in prison, stipulating that he should never be released.

Milk is Murder

Bertha House

On a chilly February morning in 1941, 69-year-old Walter Samples opened the front door of his house in Memphis, Tennessee, and spotted a bottle of milk sitting on the step. This perplexed him somewhat as he hadn't put out an empty bottle and token the previous evening and hadn't expected a delivery. Deciding that the milkman had probably made a mistake, he visited his neighbors on either side and asked if the milk belonged to them. Both said no. Samples then carried the bottle home and put it in his refrigerator, figuring that it was his lucky day.

That evening, Walter poured himself a glass of milk from the bottle and enjoyed it with his supper, suffering no ill effects. The following morning, he splashed some over his breakfast cereal and added a dollop to his coffee. This time, however, the milk did not seem to agree with him. He'd only swallowed a few spoonfuls of corn flakes when a sharp pain flared in his gut. Then another spasm racked his body, and he suddenly felt flushed and woozy. Staggering to his feet, he made his way down the passage to his bedroom, using the wall for support. He collapsed on the bed and lay there for nearly an hour, writhing in pain. Eventually, he felt his throat begin to constrict and realized that he had to get help.

Walter Samples was as tough as they come, a retired military engineer who had seen service in the Spanish-American War of 1898. But even for him, the next twenty minutes must have required superhuman effort. Somehow he managed to pull himself out of his bed, to drag himself through the house and to open the front door. He then staggered out onto the street and encountered a neighbor. "Call an ambulance," he rasped to the startled man. "Tell them I've been poisoned."

And that would turn out to be an accurate assessment. Samples was rushed to the Veterans Hospital where emergency efforts to save his life proved futile. Within four hours, he was dead with strychnine poisoning suspected. An autopsy and the subsequent analysis of the leftover milk would prove that the poison used was actually phosphorus. Someone had left a tainted bottle of milk on Walter Samples's front porch with the express intention of killing him.

The question was who? Who would want to murder a lonely old bachelor in such a horrible way? Samples was, by all accounts, a private person who was cordial with his neighbors but kept mostly to himself. He seldom, if ever, received visitors at his neat little bungalow. Neighbors described him as "quiet, almost hermit-like." Beyond the fact that he was a military veteran, no one seemed to know too much about him.

And, as is often the case when someone prefers to keep the details of their private life to themselves, there were rumors. In Walter Samples's case, those rumors were that he was actually filthy rich, having invested his military pension in rental property. There were also whisperings that he didn't trust banks and kept a small fortune in cash hidden somewhere in his house. Might this have been a motive for murder? Walter's brother Donald certainly seemed to think so, although the investigating officers were less certain. In their experience, a robber used a cosh or a pistol. No one could recall a case of burglary facilitated by poison.

A search of the dead man's residence might have cleared up the mystery. Instead it turned up more questions than answers. There was no evidence of burglary. Nor was there any hidden stockpile of cash. What the police did find was a bank book which indicated that Walter Samples had accumulated the grand total of $300 in savings. Whatever the reason for the murder, it had not been financial. It may, however, have been precipitated by that other standby motive in murder cases – sex.

Samples had been keeping secrets. The search of the house may have failed to locate his reported fortune, but it had turned up a large stash of photographs, described by lead detective M.A. Hinds as "pictures of attractive women." It appeared that the lonely, home-loving bachelor had another side to him. Apparently, he was quite the ladies' man.

This new information veered the investigation in an entirely new direction and presented the police with a mammoth challenge. Over the weeks that followed, they undertook the considerable task of tracking down all of the women in the photographs and interviewing them. Samples hadn't had a particular "type" when it came to female companionship. His lady friends were young and old, plain and attractive, married and single. Might that hint at a motive? Had some jealous husband or boyfriend decided to kill the old man over a dalliance? The police didn't think so. Poison, in their experience, was a woman's weapon. They were certain that they would find Samples's killer among his harem of lovers.

But hundreds of interviews brought them no closer to finding a suspect. All of the ladies questioned denied involvement, and many insisted that they'd been on friendly terms with Walter Samples and no more. With growing frustration, investigators began to wonder whether the murder would ever be solved.

That was until Donald Samples presented them with an interesting piece of information. While acting as executor for his brother's estate, Donald had come across an unusual transaction. In the weeks prior to Walter's death, a woman named Bertha House had paid him the sum of $7,600 (around $120,000 at current values). Donald had no idea what the payment was for.

Bertha House had not been one of the women included in Walter Samples's photograph collection. But the pretty brunette would undoubtedly have appealed to the romantically inclined bachelor. Looking into her background, detectives found that she was 36 years old and married to a trucking company executive named Louis Roy House, also 36. The couple was apparently well off and owned the 1,300-acre Green Acres Plantation on the outskirts of Columbus, Mississippi.

Digging deeper, however, showed a different picture. The Houses
had bought the plantation for $45,000 in October 1940, putting
down a small down payment and raising a mortgage for the rest.
But they were soon in arrears, and the bank was on the verge of
foreclosing when they suddenly came up with the shortfall. Now
they were facing foreclosure again, and as any detective knows,
financial pressure can drive even the most law-abiding citizen to
do reckless things. It was time to speak to Mrs. House.

Bertha House had no problem in admitting that she had known
Walter Samples. She said that she'd met him over a decade earlier
when she had been selling washing machines for a living and he
had bought one from her. "He was a dear old friend," she said. "I
was deeply saddened to hear of his death." She also did not try to
conceal the fact that Walter had helped her out of a "tight spot"
financially. The $7,600 had been a repayment on the loan, she said,
adding that her husband knew nothing about. Asked outright
whether she'd had anything to do with his death, Mrs. House
appeared outraged and vehemently denied it.

And that left the police in somewhat of a quandary. Being unable
to repay the money she owed might have provided Mrs. House
with a motive. But she had repaid at least part of the loan in the
weeks before Samples died. Why do that if she was planning on
killing him to extricate herself from her financial commitments?
That question was answered when the police searched the
property and found a will, purportedly made by W.L. Samples and
leaving his entire estate to Bertha House. This document would
prove to be a forgery.

But here the case takes yet another unusual twist. Before an arrest warrant could be issued for Mrs. House, her husband Louis came forward to confess to the crime. According to Louis, it was he who had left the poisoned milk on the doorstep. His wife, he insisted had had nothing to do with it. His act of gallantry would, however, go unrewarded. On April 11, 1941, the Shelby County grand jury handed down murder indictments to both of the Houses.

Bertha and Louis House went to trial in September 1942 and were both convicted of murder and sentenced to 20 years in prison.

But the story doesn't end there.

A year later, the Tennessee Supreme Court overturned the convictions, ruling that Louis House's confession had been improperly introduced at trial. That meant that the matter would have to be brought before the courts again, but before that could happen, Bertha contacted prosecutors and said that she wanted to confess. She now admitted that it was she who had poisoned the milk and left it outside Walter Samples's house. She'd done it in order to free herself from her debt to him. She had also hoped to inherit his estate, but his death had caused such a stir that she had been afraid to present the forged will for fear of arousing suspicion.

Bertha House entered a guilty plea at her second trial. She was re-sentenced to 20 years in prison.

In the Name of Lust

Victor Miller

On a frigid afternoon in January 1988, 18-year-old Richard Holden was riding his bicycle along the already darkened streets of Wellington, in the West Midlands county of Herefordshire, England. Richard had just turned onto a quiet country lane when he spotted a small, silver car at the roadside with its lights on. He was approaching the vehicle when a man got out of the driver's seat and held up a hand, bringing him to a stop. The strongly-built stranger then said that he was lost and asked for directions. But before Richard even had a chance to reply, he drew a knife and held it to the startled teenager's throat. "Do what I say and you won't get hurt," he growled.

Richard was caught totally by surprise, unable to respond. He was forced from his bike and marched at knifepoint into the bushes. There, with the blade still held to his throat, he was ordered to remove his clothes. It was at that point that he decided to fight back, spinning away from his assailant and aiming a kick at his groin. The man then turned and ran back in the direction of his car.

Richard heard the engine turn over and the wheels spin on tarmac as he raced away.

Richard Holden reported the incident to the police, saying that his attacker was a black man of medium height driving a small silver sedan. Just days later, a man matching that description was involved in another attempted abduction in nearby Hagley, Worcestershire.

The intended victim was 14-year-old Anthony Dingley who had a newspaper route in the town. Dingley had been making his deliveries when he was stopped by a black man driving a silver car. The man said that he was lost and needed directions to Birmingham. He then tried to strike up a conversation with Anthony, although the teenager was wary of his overly friendly manner. He eventually told the man that he had to go as he was running late. Thereafter, the man seemed to be tailing him, reappearing four times along his newspaper route. Frightened, Anthony eventually decided to hide and took cover in some bushes. While he was there, he saw the silver vehicle drift slowly by, the driver obviously looking for something or someone. Later that evening, a 25-year-old woman reported to police that she had been out walking her dog when a man driving a silver Datsun Sunny had stopped and punched her in the face before driving off.

On the morning after Anthony Dingley's terrifying encounter with the motorist, another delivery boy walked into the general store run by Malcolm Higgins and his wife in Hagley. Like Anthony Dingley, Stuart Gough was 14 years old and working a newspaper route to earn extra pocket money. The Higgins's store served as the center of operations, where the delivery boys picked up their papers. Stuart had fourteen drops to make that morning, all of them within a few hundred yards of the store. He grabbed his first batch of newspapers, saying that he'd return shortly for the others. He never did.

Store owner Malcolm Higgins was aware that Stuart Gough suffered from asthma. So when Stuart failed to return to the store as promised, Higgins became concerned that he might have suffered an attack. He went looking for the boy, walking his delivery route but finding no trace of him. It also did not take long before he realized that Stuart had made only his first few deliveries. Higgins then walked back to his store and called the police.

A search was initiated that day, one that grew into the largest ever carried out by the West Mercia police. Hagley, with a population of just over 6,000, quickly became the focus of national media attention as 150 police officers and 600 volunteers worked the area, looking for any trace of the missing boy. They were assisted in their effort by mounted police, dogs, an underwater search unit, and even a helicopter with thermal imaging cameras. Unfortunately, they came up empty. The area surrounding Hagley is vast and includes the rugged Clent Hills as well as several bodies of water. Despite a concerted effort, a house-to-house search of the village and an appeal for information which included a re-enactment of Stuart's last movements, the boy remained a missing person.

Detectives, meanwhile, had picked up on an important clue, the driver of a silver Datsun who had been involved in two assaults and an attempted abduction in the days leading up to Stuart's disappearance. Might this man be linked to the missing boy? Investigators considered it a strong possibility. Descriptions of the man and his vehicle were therefore distributed to police forces in the area. Two weeks later, it paid off when a 32-year-old warehouse worker from Penn Fields, Wolverhampton was arrested on an unrelated charge.

Victor Miller didn't drive a Datsun Sunny, but he did drive a silver Colt Sappora, which closely resembles the Datsun. He was also a convicted pedophile. Back in 1980, he had been convicted of kidnapping and sexually assaulting a 13-year-old boy. He had served seven years for that crime.

Although Miller was flagged as the prime suspect in the disappearance of Stuart Gough, the police made no effort to charge him at this point. They first wanted to build a case against him. A key piece of evidence was obtained when crime scene technicians took impressions of tire tracks found at the suspected abduction site and compared them to the tires on Miller's vehicle. It was a match. That proved that Miller had been in the area, but proving that he had been there when Stuart went missing would be a more difficult task. Miller had an alibi, provided by his lover, Trevor Peacher. According to Peacher, Miller had been at home with him on the morning that Stuart Gough disappeared.

It was a blow to the investigation but not an insurmountable one. Trevor Peacher could hardly be described as a reliable witness.

Like his lover, he was a convicted sex criminal with an extensive rap sheet for assaults on juvenile boys. It was not a stretch to imagine that he was lying. On January 27, the police decided to see how deep his loyalty to Miller ran. Both men were arrested on suspicion of murder. Four days later, Victor Miller cracked and admitted that it was he, and he alone, who had abducted, raped, and murdered Stuart Gough.

According to Miller, he and Peacher had argued that morning, and he'd left their apartment seething with anger. He'd then decided to abduct and rape a boy in revenge and had driven to Hadley, an area he had trawled before. He said that he targeted newspaper boys because they were "vulnerable." After spotting Stuart, he'd stopped him, ostensibly to ask for directions. Instead, he'd forced the boy into his car, driven him to an isolated spot and raped him. He'd then decided to cover up his crime by killing his young victim. Stuart had been clubbed to death with a rock.

The following morning, February 1, 1988, a convoy of police vehicles left Hereford police station and were directed by Miller to an area near the village of Bromsberrow, some 40 miles south of Hagley along the M50 motorway. There, lying in a drainage culvert, covered by leaves, they found Stuart Gough's partially-clothed body. The cold weather had delayed decomposition, so it was clear to see the savage injuries that had been inflicted on his head and face. The boy who had so diligently performed his part-time job in an effort to raise pocket money had suffered a horrible death.

It is hard to find any redeeming qualities in a man like Victor Miller. But Miller did, at least, take responsibility for his horrendous deeds. At his first court appearance, before Hereford Magistrates Court, Miller had made it clear that he did not intend to defend the charges against him. He also asked to be given the maximum sentence available under the law. That wish was granted went he was sentenced to life imprisonment with a minimum of 25 years to be served before he is eligible for parole. The sentence was later increased to a 'whole life tariff' by the Home Secretary, which means that Miller will die behind bars.

Trevor Peacher was later convicted of 'perverting the cause of justice' for providing Miller with a false alibi. He received a three-year jail sentence.

Death on a Spring Day

The city of Cumberland is a picturesque burg situated in the
Appalachian Mountains of western Maryland. Once it was an
important locale for the coal mining, iron ore, and timber
industries as well as a major railroad junction. That had allowed it
to grow to the second largest metro in the state, reaching its peak
population in 1940. By the mid-sixties, however, the boom was
over, and Cumberland's population had declined to around 31,000.
Still, it was a pleasant place to live. Jean Welch certainly thought
so.

The attractive brunette lived in an apartment on Oldtown Road
with her husband and three young daughters. An upbeat person by
nature, Jean had particular reason to feel happy on the afternoon
of May 17, 1965. Spring had been tardy in its arrival, but today it
was here in all its glory. It was a perfect, sunny day for hanging
laundry, and that is exactly what Jean intended doing. Her winter
clothes stashed away, she strolled into the backyard dressed in
shorts and a light blouse, carrying her laundry basket. She had no
inkling at all that someone was watching her.

At around 4 p.m. that afternoon, Jean's 13-year-old daughter, Judy,
arrived home from school and entered the apartment, using the
side door on New Hampshire Avenue. She found the place in a
mess, which was most unusual. Her mother was an excellent
housekeeper and a stickler for tidiness. Judy could also hear her
two-year-old sister, Loy Lee, crying somewhere in the apartment.
That too was unusual. Jean doted on the girls.

"Mom?" Judy called out.

No answer. But for Loy Lee's pitiful cries, the apartment was quiet. Judy felt gooseflesh creep up her arms. For no apparent reason, she suddenly felt the urge to turn around and flee the apartment. Were it not for her sister's crying, she would likely have done just that. Instead, she walked to the back bedroom where she found Loy Lee and her younger sister, Dee Dee. Calming the children down, she asked Loy Lee where their mother was. All that did was trigger a fresh flood of tears from the child.

Judy was by now certain that something had happened to their mother, something bad. Her instinct was to take her sisters and get out of the apartment, but the brave little girl instead carried out a search of the house. Perhaps her mother had fallen and was hurt. "Mom!" she called out, more anxiously this time. No answer came. Judy walked to her mother's bedroom and found it empty. Next, she rapped her fingers on the closed door of the bathroom. "Mom, are you in there?" Nothing. Judy twisted the handle and pushed the door inward. In the next moment, she was turning, running, screaming at the top of her voice.

Dale Welch had spent that Monday afternoon enjoying a round of golf with some clients at the Cumberland Country Club. Dale was the VP of Sales for the Air-Flow Roofing and Siding Company, and so he had a two-way radio in his car, allowing him to stay in touch with the office. He was on his way back there when the radio squawked into life. "Dale, I think you'd better get back home," a secretary informed him. "There's a problem with Jean."

That, as it turned out, was a major understatement. Dale arrived home to find a small fleet of police cars parked on Oldtown Road and several officers trying to keep a crowd of onlookers at bay. Those same officers prevented Dale from entering until a detective had taken him aside and talked to him. "It's bad news," the officer said in a practiced tone. He then went on to explain that Jean had been attacked, beaten on the head with a blunt instrument, strangled with a drapery cord, and then drowned in the bathtub.

Cumberland is generally a low crime city. Violent offenses are rare and murders rarer still. The local police were ill-equipped to handle an investigation of this magnitude. It was therefore decided from the outset to assign the case to a task team, with state and county investigators working alongside detectives of the Cumberland Police Department. Ten officers were seconded to work full-time on the investigation, and they got to work immediately, knocking on doors and questioning neighbors, speaking to friends and relatives of the victim. Within a week, more than 300 people had been interviewed, and still the police knew very little. A neighbor had seen Jean hanging laundry at around 1:30 p.m.; a couple living across the street from the Welch residence had noticed that the drapes were closed that afternoon, which they thought unusual on such a beautiful, sunny day; a woman who was at home in an upstairs apartment reported hearing nothing unusual, despite what must have been a violent, life-and-death struggle going on beneath her feet.

Two other pieces of information were worth considering. The couple who'd spotted the closed drapes had spent the afternoon sitting on their porch and had seen no one enter or leave via the Oldtown Road entrance. The upstairs neighbor had, however, heard a knock at the side door of the Welch's apartment at around 2 p.m. That entrance was on New Hampshire Avenue and was used only by friends and family.

The police, meanwhile, were having no luck finding the weapon that had been used to beat Jean Welch. Since nothing of that kind was missing from the Welch residence, they assumed that the killer must have brought it with him and left with it in hand. He might also have discarded it nearby, and the police expended considerable effort in trying to find it. It might, after all, contain fingerprints or other forensic evidence. The search, however, would come up empty. Despite hundreds of man-hours spent trawling through trash cans, vacant lots, sewers, and construction sites, the weapon was never found.

And then there was motive. Since nothing had been taken from the house, robbery could safely be ruled out. Was this a sex crime? If Jean had been raped, the police weren't saying so. Might she have been killed in some sort of revenge attack? That did not seem likely since Jean appeared to have been universally liked, with no known enemies. There might also have been another motive, of course. Dale Welch might have killed his wife, for either financial gain or personal reasons.

When a married person is killed, the surviving spouse is always the first suspect. There is a good reason for this. In the vast majority of cases, it turns out to be the partner who did it. But Dale Welch had been miles away, at the Cumberland Country Club, at the time of the murder. His golfing buddies could vouch for that. Besides, Dale had no obvious motive. His wife had only a small life insurance policy, and their marriage was, by all accounts, a happy one. They did not have financial problems and neither of them had been conducting an extra-marital affair. Dale Welch was thus dismissed as a suspect, at least in the eyes of the police.

The good people of Cumberland, though, saw things differently. Wild rumors began circulating, naming Dale as the killer. These stories became so virulent that the state's attorney took the unusual step of warning members of the public that they left themselves open to legal action if they continued to defame an innocent man. Yet the stories persisted, even after Welch volunteered to take a polygraph and passed on two separate occasions. He would go to his death years later with the stain of suspicion still hanging over his head.

The murder of Jean Welch was never solved, in part because the police did such a poor job of processing of the crime scene. Vital clues were missed, and important evidence, including blood samples and fingerprints, were lost due to mishandling. The obsession with information gathering also backfired, since the small team lacked the capacity to process the deluge of data. Aside from that, there was a serious lack of co-ordination. Rather than ten detectives working together to solve the crime, there were ten detectives, each of whom was more or less conducting his own investigation. In the end, the inquiry collapsed under the weight of its own haphazard efforts.

So who killed Jean Welch? At the time of the investigation, the police chief suggested (rather redundantly) that it was either a friend, a family member or a transient. The latter can probably be discounted. Jean would have been unlikely to admit a stranger to her home, and a stranger would have been unlikely to knock at the side door. There was also no evidence of a struggle, either in the yard or on the doorstep. Might Jean have allowed a male friend in? Probably not. It would have been unusual, during that era, for a respectable married woman to entertain a male guest while her husband was not at home.

That narrows the field to a member of Jean's family, and many of the pieces start to fit into place once you consider it from that angle. A family member would have used the side entrance, and Jean would have had no problem letting him in. She would also have been off guard, making an attack from behind, using a bludgeon, more likely to succeed. What motive might this assailant have had? The one that the police had been unwilling to discuss, a sexual motive. More than likely, he had developed an obsession with Jean, an obsession that built over time until he felt compelled to act on it.

This is more than just supposition. During the early 2000s, cold case investigators from the state's attorney office took another look at the surviving forensic evidence. Their findings were never made public, although a leak revealed that they had identified the killer but lacked sufficient proof to secure a murder conviction. According to the source, Jean Welch's killer was indeed a member of her family who was still alive at the time of the cold case investigation. That rules out Dale Welch, since he had already passed away by then. The case remains officially unsolved.

A Monster Among Us

To naïve 17-year-old June, the attention of local bad boy Rab Thomson was flattering. Thomson had a reputation for violence around the small Scottish town of Kilbirnie. At age 19, he already had a record for assault and for various public order offenses. But to June, he was nothing but charming. It wasn't long before she'd fallen hopelessly in love with him.

The early part of the relationship was a happy time for the couple. Despite his notoriously quick temper, Rab held down a good job in construction and was a diligent worker. June soon learned that he was obsessed with status and wanted everything of the best, the best clothes, the best car. She also saw first-hand how quickly he could go from quiet and pleasant to angry and explosive. On one occasion, he smashed a glass in the face of a friend after the man had made an innocent comment that Rab disapproved of; on another, he attacked a motorist, throttling him in front of his wife. It wasn't long, either, before he turned his aggression on his teenaged girlfriend.

It started in the form of control. Rab expected June to dress in a certain way and to wear no make-up, not even nail varnish. "Only whores paint their nails," he told her. Once, when June wore an outfit he felt was inappropriate, he ordered her to change it immediately, threatening that he'd tear it off her if she failed to comply. And then came the day when he used physical violence against June for the first time. It came after she returned the greeting of a male work colleague. That earned her a slap across the face and a warning that "there was more where that came from" if she ever again "flirted" with another man. June was shocked by the attack, but later, on reflection, she felt almost flattered. Rab must love her a lot if a simple wave to another man threw him into a jealous rage.

In 1981, after dating for two years, Rab asked June to marry him. Or rather, he told her that they were getting married. It wasn't so much a proposal as a decree. Still, June had no objection. She was very much in love with her broody boyfriend and thought that marriage might calm him down. Perhaps if they were married, he wouldn't be so insecure about their relationship; perhaps he'd start treating her like a partner, rather than a possession.

But June was wrong. Marriage only made Rab more controlling. First he moved her away from her hometown and set up home 80 miles away in Buckhaven, on Scotland's east coast. Then he began cutting her off from her family. When June's sister phoned to speak to her one day, he told her never to call again and hung up the phone. Meanwhile, he was becoming increasingly demanding at home. After June fell pregnant and quit her job, he would make up a schedule of things for her to do during the day. When he returned from work at night, he'd carry out a military style inspection, even running his hand along the tops of doors to check for dust. Woe betide June if anything did not meet his exacting standards. She'd suffer a vicious beating, followed often by a violent rape.

And then came the night when Thomson came home drunk and attacked his heavily pregnant wife for no reason other than the one he gave. "You're useless," he snarled before pushing her so hard that she was sent tumbling down a flight of stairs. Miraculously, June escaped without serious injury. For her unborn child, though, the result of that attack was catastrophic. Michelle would be born with severe learning disabilities and would require special care throughout her life.

Two more children followed over the next four years, Shaun in 1983 and Ross, born in 1985. But while Rab appeared to dote on the children and was indeed a good provider for his family, his aggression towards June only seemed to escalate. She was branded "useless, stupid, and lazy," regularly beaten and just as frequently raped. The only reason June endured was because of her children. What would become of them if she left Rab? She did not have a job anymore, she owned nothing, she didn't even have a bank account.

It would be no exaggeration to say that June Thomson would have suffered any indignity to keep her children safe. But as they grew older, their safety was no longer a forgone conclusion. As Rab had sought to control his wife, now he turned his attention to his growing sons. Ross and (especially) Shaun were frequently beaten, often over the most trivial infraction. Their father's preferred weapon was a belt buckle which left such obvious bruises that the boys sometimes had to stay home from school. It was this escalating level of violence against her children that eventually persuaded June to leave Rab. One night she simply packed up the kids while Rab was out and checked in at a hostel for battered women.

June might have expected a violent response from Rab for this "desertion" but instead he resorted to manipulation. Eventually, after weeks of telling her how much he missed her and the children, she caved in and allowed them to visit. That turned out to be a mistake. Rab immediately abducted the children and took them out of the country, to Ireland. From there, he contacted June and told her that she would never see her children again unless she came back to him. Placed in an impossible situation, she agreed.

For Rab, everything was now as it should be. He'd resumed control of his fiefdom, and June was back to being his slave and punching bag. The children, too, were reacquainted with their father's unique brand of parental control. Aside from being Rab's cook and housekeeper, June was also his sex slave, obliged to submit to his sexual demands whenever the urge took him. As a result, she fell pregnant again and, at 41, she gave birth to another son who the couple named Ryan.

Perhaps in Ryan, there was an opportunity to mend this fractured family. The boy was adored by both his parents, universally loved by his three siblings. But his presence in the household did nothing to temper Rab Thomson's malevolent persona. Eventually, Shaun had had enough and left to join the army. June, too, was rapidly reaching the point of no return.

The final straw came when Rab started threatening to send Michelle to a care home. That was when June decided that enough was enough. She moved with Michelle and Ryan to rented accommodation and started divorce proceedings. At the hearing on May 2, 2008, she was given full custody of the children, and Rab was allowed access visits. That same night, he phoned his son Shaun, now living in Essex, and urged him to return to Scotland to "talk sense" into his mother. Shaun declined and assured him that June was never coming back to him.

The next day, May 3, 2008, Michelle and Ryan were due to visit their father at the family home, under the terms of the custody arrangement. June dropped them off at around 3:30 p.m., secure in the knowledge that Rab had never been violent to either child and that her other son, Ross, now 20, was also in the house. When she left that day, she had no idea that it would be the last time that she would see either Michelle or Ryan alive.

For Rab Thompson had planned a horrific revenge on the estranged wife. Once Michelle was in her room, once Ross had retired to watch a DVD, once Ryan was quietly playing video games on his computer, Rab went down to the kitchen and fetched a large knife. He visited Ryan first, launching a brutal attack during which he plunged the knife fourteen times into the little boy he professed to love. Next, he went to Michelle's room, attacking her as she lay on the bed, inflicting twelve wounds, many of them to the hands and arms as Michelle tried in vain to defend herself.

Having killed his two most vulnerable children, Thomson tucked both of them up in bed before making a half-hearted attempt at suicide, swallowing a handful of Michelle's epilepsy pills and inflicting superficial wounds to his wrists. He left behind a suicide note in which he'd written: "Ross – goodbye, son. Thanks when I needed you, love dad. June – too much pain, lies and hurt. Don't blame yourself. I will look after them. Just like your mother, move on alone. Shaun – bye, son, had to take a holiday. Love, Rab XXX."

Ross had been watching a movie through headphones in his room at the time of the murders and was totally oblivious to the carnage. It was left to June to find her butchered children. She arrived hours later and found the house eerily silent. She then went up to Ryan's room and found him lying under the covers in his bed, his mouth open, his lips blue, not even the faintest breath left in him. Her screams attracted the attention of Ross who called the police.

Ryan and Michelle Thomson were both pronounced dead at the scene. Their killer, meanwhile, was transported to a nearby hospital for treatment to his superficial wounds. He was then taken to the police station for questioning where he proved to be an uncooperative and callous witness who showed not a modicum of concern for his dead children.

Rab Thomson ultimately pled guilty to the murder of Ryan and Michelle and was sentenced to life imprisonment with no parole for at least 17 years. Most commentators, including the murdered children's mother, considered that sentence to be wholly inadequate.

Thomson, however, seemed to believe that he had been hard done by. After convincing June to visit him in prison, on the pretense of explaining what he'd done, he launched into a tirade in which he blamed her for the death of their children. "I didn't kill them, you did it," he insisted. He then urged her to stop this "divorce nonsense," as though there was still a chance that they might have a future together. It was at that point that June got up and walked away, never to return.

Cabin 28

The town of Keddie had seen better days. Once it had been a thriving resort of quaint log cabins set in the picturesque foothills of the Sierra Nevada Mountains. It had also been an important stop on the rail route between Salt Lake City and Oakland, California. But by 1981, the railroad was gone, the tourists were gone, and all that remained was a collection of ramshackle wooden bungalows, occupied by low-income families. Still it was a quiet town, a peaceful town, a town where the worst that Sheriff Doug Thomas had to deal with was the reputed over-indulgence by some residents in marijuana and hashish.

Single mom Glenna "Sue" Sharp had come to Keddie for the same reason as many of the town's citizens. Rent was cheap, and with five mouths to feed, every cent was important. And so Sue had leased Cabin 28 and settled in with her children – Johnny, 15, Sheila, 14, Tina, 12, Ricky, 10, and Greg, the youngest, who was five years of age. Things weren't exactly peachy, but her kids had a roof over their heads and food on their plates. Sue's biggest problem was that her eldest son had taken to hanging out with a local mischief-maker, 17-year-old Dana Wingate.

Sue Sharp kept mostly to herself in Keddie. Her closest friend was a woman named Marilyn Smartt who lived at Cabin 26 with her husband, Marty, and two sons. One of the boys, Justin, was a friend of Sue's son Ricky, and so the two women struck up an acquaintanceship. But it wasn't just their kids that had drawn them together. As the survivor of a bad marriage, Sue had immediately noticed the signs of abuse in Marilyn, the beaten-down demeanor, the bruises, the sudden lapses into tears. Lately, Marilyn had been talking to Sue about leaving Marty, and Sue had provided a shoulder to cry on. She hadn't outright encouraged Marilyn to walk out on her marriage, but she had told her that divorcing her ex had been one of the best decisions she'd ever made. It was an obscure piece of advice at best. It would end up costing Sue Sharp her life.

On the evening of April 11, 1981, Marilyn arranged for her son, Justin, to sleep over with his friend Ricky Sharp. There was plenty of room in the Sharps' bungalow that night. Sheila was staying with a friend, while Johnny had gone to the nearby town of Quincy with Dana Wingate. Sue wasn't exactly thrilled about that, but Johnny was 15 now and more or less a law unto himself. As she settled her other kids down for the night and then retired herself, she said a silent prayer that he would stay out of trouble. She was always on edge when he was out with Dana.

Early the next morning, Sheila Sharp returned to Cabin 28 from her sleepover. As she walked up the path, she was surprised to see lights on in the living room. It was a Sunday, after all. She'd expected that the family would be sleeping in. But the mystery of the glowing lights was unraveled the minute she opened the front door. That was when she was confronted by the sight of her mother lying on the floor. Sue Sharp was covered with a yellow blanket, but the blood that had seeped into the fabric left no doubt that she had been gravely hurt. Not that Sheila registered that fact immediately. The mind plays strange tricks in situations such as these, and the device it most commonly uses is disbelief. There was her mother under the bloodstained blanket, and there, a short distance away, was her brother Johnny and his friend Dana, their feet bound together with electrical cable. The blood that fouled their bodies had splattered up onto the walls and furnishings. And there was a knife lying on the floor, a steak knife with a bent blade that was drenched in gore. Sheila took all of this in before the horror of it struck home. Then she was turning, running blindly back to her friend's house, her screams punctuating the still morning air.

Sheriff Doug Thomas, along with several deputies of Plumas County Sheriff's Department, were soon on the scene. And almost immediately, they started making mistakes. They failed to secure the crime scene, left their boot prints in the victims' blood, handled evidence without gloves. Still, we should not judge the Sheriff and his men too harshly. Most of them had never dealt with a murder before, let alone a triple homicide of this savagery. Sue Sharp had been stabbed multiple times, the wounds inflicted with such ferocity that the blade of the murder weapon had bent by almost 25 degrees. The male victims had also been stabbed in what looked like a frenzied attack. Additionally, Dana Wingate had been bludgeoned. The deep, circular indentations on his skull suggested that the killer had used a hammer on him.

By this point, some of the officers looked as though they might run from the scene and throw up in the woods. But there was still the house to be searched, other potential victims to be found. Sheila Sharp had informed them that her sister and brothers were still in the house. Fearing the worst, the officers began going through the rooms one by one. It was in the rear bedroom that they found Ricky, Greg, and Justin Smartt, miraculously, unhurt.

Of Tina, though, there was no trace, and here the Sheriff's Department made another mistake. They were slow to launch a search for the missing girl and were cursory (at best) in their efforts. Sheriff Thomas had already decided that his department was not equipped to deal with a crime of this magnitude. He placed a call to the California Department of Justice and asked for help from the Bureau of Criminal Identification and Investigation.

With three surviving eyewitnesses, this should have been an easy crime to solve. But the boys turned out to be no help at all. Ricky and Greg claimed to have slept through the whole thing, while Justin kept changing his story. First, he said that he had slept through the ordeal, then he claimed that he had seen the killers, then he said that he might have seen them "in a dream." The most likely scenario was that the boys had seen something but were so traumatized that they had shut it out.

What then of the neighbors? The cabins in Keddie are spaced closely together. Surely someone must have heard the screams of the victims? Apparently not. Only one neighbor reported hearing anything and was still uncertain whether it had been a woman screaming or the screech of an owl.

But while no one appeared to have heard screams coming from Cabin 28, one of the neighbors had seen someone calling at the property on the night of the murder. Marty Smartt, his wife Marilyn, and their houseguest Bo Boubede had been seen knocking at Sue Sharp's front door at around nine that evening.

Brought in for questioning, the trio confirmed their visit. They had gone to ask Sue to join them for drinks at a local bar, they said. Sue had declined and they'd left – end of story. That, at least, was the story told by Marty and Bo. Marilyn had more to tell. She said that they had barely arrived at the bar when Marty had gotten into an angry confrontation with the owner over the music that was playing. The three of them had then left and returned to their cabin. When Marty and Bo went out again a short while later, Marilyn had decided to stay behind. She had watched some TV and then gone to bed. She had not seen her husband or his friend until the next morning. And then Marilyn added something else. She said that Marty had harbored a grudge against Sue Sharp, who he believed had been advising her to divorce him.

This potential motive should have immediately elevated Marty Smartt to the top of the suspect list. The reason it didn't has been the subject of much conjecture. Some put it down to incompetence by the Plumas County Sheriff's Department while others suggest something more sinister. Marty Smartt and Sheriff Doug Thomas were close friends. In fact, it would later be revealed that Marty had been a long-term houseguest in the Sheriff's home in the months after the murders. During that time, Thomas inexplicably quit law enforcement. His next job would be selling insurance.

That, however, was in the future. For now, two agents from the California Bureau of Criminal Identification and Investigation (CII) had arrived, and Sheriff Thomas had passed the reins to them. The investigation was in professional hands at last. Or was it? In retrospect, the CII agents appear to have made even more mistakes than the bungling Sheriff Thomas. For starters, they accepted Bo Boubede's story that he was a retired police officer (a lie) at face value. Thereafter, they treated him with a deference bordering on hero worship. As a result, they ignored several glaring contradictions in the statements given by Boubede and by Marty Smartt.

At the start of his interview, for example, Boubede admitted that he knew which cabin the murder had been committed in. Later, he said that he did not know which one it was. He also stated on record that he had never met Sue Sharp, even though he had called at her cabin on the night of the murders. And he said that he and Marty had left the bar at midnight, having previously told Sheriff Thomas that they'd left between 9:30 and 10 p.m. He told other lies, too. He said that Marilyn was his niece when they were not related; he said that he'd been in Keddie for a month when, in fact, he'd only been there 12 days; he said that Marilyn was awake when he and Marty got home when Marilyn had already told investigators that she was asleep.

As for the interrogation of Marty Smartt, it was so badly executed that it verged on farce. At one point during the interview, Smartt admitted that he thought his son Justin might have seen something "... without me detecting him..." This remark suggests that Marty was inside the Smartt house where his son was sleeping over. It directly implicates him in the murders. The agents chose not to follow it up. Neither did they make anything of his unsolicited comment that his hammer had recently "gone missing." A hammer had, of course, been used to kill Dana Wingate.

Even the greenest of detectives would have picked up on these discrepancies, but for some reason, the experienced CII agents let them slide. They then compounded their shoddy work by allowing their main suspects to leave town. Bo Boubede went back to the VA hospital in Reno, Nevada, where he had been receiving treatment for Post-Traumatic Stress Disorder; Marty Smartt, now separated from his wife Marilyn, moved to Klamath, California.

With the investigation so badly bungled, it is perhaps unsurprising that this thoroughly solvable case went cold. It soon disappeared from the news and remained so until 1984, when a human skull was found at Feather Falls, some 29 miles from Keddie. It was later matched by DNA to Tina Sharp, making this a quadruple homicide.

The next development in the case came when Marty Smartt died in 2000, and his therapist revealed that he had been treating Marty and that Marty had confessed the murders to him. According to the therapist, Marty said that he had killed Sue Sharp due to her "interference" in his marriage. He did not confess to killing Dana, Johnny or Tina, which suggests that Bo Boubede might have been responsible for those murders. But Bo would never be held to account. He'd died of natural causes in 1988. Three decades on, and the Keddie Cabin killings remain officially unsolved.

FOOTNOTE: In the aftermath of the murders, there was a mass exodus from Keddie. Only a small number of the homes in the town remain occupied, and Cabin 28 is not one of them. It was bulldozed into the ground in 2004.

Ultimate Betrayal

Hann Pan and his wife Bich Ha had come to Canada in 1979.
They'd come as political refugees, ethnic Chinese fleeing a
repressive regime in Vietnam, "Vietnamese Boat People," in the
somewhat insensitive parlance of the time. Hann and Bich had
arrived in Toronto with not much more than the clothes on their
backs; neither of them had been able to speak English. But what
Hann and Bich did possess was a fierce work ethic. By 2004, the
long hours they'd put in at the auto parts factory where they both
worked, the scrimping and saving, had paid off. They were living
the dream in the comfortable suburb of Markham. Parked in their
two-car garage was a Lexus ES 300 for Bich and a Mercedes-Benz
for Hann. Their saving account balance, at that time, stood at
$200,000 (Canadian).

If ever there was a story to illustrate the benefits of immigration, it
was that of the Pans. But the couple had not accumulated their
fortune for the sake of wealth itself. Their main concern was for
their children, Jennifer, born in 1986, and Felix, born in 1989. They

wanted to ensure that the kids were given every opportunity to make a success of their lives.

Asian parents are notoriously hard taskmasters who push their children to excel academically, at sports, and in the arts. And the Pans were no exception, especially with daughter, Jennifer. Beginning piano lessons at the age of four, she showed an early talent for music. She also excelled at figure skating, and her parents hoped that she might one day be an Olympian until a knee ligament injury put paid to that dream. Meanwhile, Jennifer's academic performance was excellent. She was a Straight-A student at Mary Ward Catholic School, where she also played the flute in the school band. These results did not come about by accident. Jennifer was sent for extra lessons from an early age. By the time she reached high school, she would be up until midnight most nights, studying and doing homework.

This hectic schedule, of course, left the now teenaged Jennifer with very little time for a social life. Not that it mattered. Her parents forbade her from dating or attending parties. She was picked up from school every day and driven directly to extra lessons or music classes. Her extracurricular activities were carefully monitored. In short, she was not allowed to spend time on anything that would not deliver some benefit further down the line.

Felix Pan was subjected to the same pressures as his sister, but while Felix seemed to excel in the cauldron of expectation, the pressure had begun to tell on Jennifer. By the 9th Grade, she was no longer the star academic of her earlier years. She still maintained a respectable 70% average, but Jennifer knew that that would not be good enough for her parents.

And so Jennifer started lying. She also became an amateur forger, altering her report cards so that they reflected the kind of grades her parents expected of her. And those lies soon grew, taking on a life of their own. When Jennifer failed a calculus class in her senior year and was denied admission to Ryerson University, she simply forged an acceptance letter and proudly showed it to her parents. Then she secretly dropped out of high school and started spending her days hanging out in coffee shops and fast food restaurants.

That deception would continue into the next year. While Jennifer's parents believed that she was attending university, she was actually earning money as a piano teacher and waitressing at a pizza parlor. The money she earned from those jobs allowed her to buy second-hand pharmacology textbooks to add an extra level of authenticity to her ruse. When Hann asked why the university had never billed him for tuition fees, Jennifer told him that is was because her excellent academic results had earned her a full scholarship. She then showed her father a letter from the University of Toronto, offering her a placement on its prestigious pharmacology program. Hann could not have been prouder.

The letter, of course, was a fake. And it wasn't the only lie that Jennifer had been spinning her parents. After telling them that she needed to live closer to the university during the week, Jennifer had been granted permission to stay with a friend and fellow student. In fact, she was spending her weeknights with Daniel

Wong, a young man she knew from high school, who was now a small-time criminal and drug dealer.

Who knows how long Jennifer might have kept up the deception, and who knows why she chose to keep it up in the first place. Jennifer was 22 years old now, legally an adult. She did not need her parents' permission for anything. She could easily have told them that she had no interest in attending university and that she would date whomever she pleased. Instead, she chose to continue with the lies. She even added a new one, saying that she had volunteered at Toronto's Hospital for Sick Children as part of her study program.

This, however, proved to be one lie too far. Jennifer had been very careful in constructing her earlier deceptions, but with this one she was lax. Hann and Bich soon began wondering why she never brought home a hospital uniform and didn't have an I.D. tag. Eventually, Bich decided to follow her daughter to work, and that was when Jennifer's intricate web of lies unraveled.

The Pans were stunned to discover that their daughter, who they thought was on the verge of earning a university degree, had not even finished high school. Hann, in fact, was so furious that he wanted to disinherit Jennifer and throw her out of the house. It was only the pleading of his wife that swayed him from that path. Jennifer could stay, but only under strict conditions. She would have to finish high school and then apply to university. She was forbidden from seeing Daniel Wong and from leaving the house for any reason other than to go to her piano-teaching job. Jennifer

meekly submitted to these demands, although she secretly
continued to see Wong.

What was it that eventually pushed Jennifer over the edge, that led
her to contemplate the murder of her parents? It might well have
been her deteriorating relationship with Daniel. The couple now
had very little opportunity to spend time together, and Wong soon
tired of the situation. He started dating another woman, much to
Jennifer's dismay. In a desperate ploy, she invented a story about
being gang-raped by a group of men who had broken into her
house. And it worked. Whether out of sympathy or concern, Wong
was back on her side. That was in the spring of 2010, and it was at
around this time that Jennifer first floated the idea of killing her
parents. Their deaths would bring her an inheritance of $500,000,
she said. She and Wong could then move in together and live a life
of luxury, no more curfews, no more sneaking around. Wong, of
course, was interested.

But who would carry out the murder? Jennifer had no intention of
killing her parents herself, and Wong, despite his tough guy act,
wasn't up to the task. What they needed was a hitman, and Wong
thought that he knew just the guy. Lenford Crawford (street name:
Homeboy) was a small-time criminal of Jamaican origin.
Approached by Wong, he immediately said that he'd take the job
but insisted that he'd need help. The men he recruited were David
Mylvaganam, born in Montreal to a Sri Lankan father and a
Jamaican mother; and Eric Carty, a drug dealer who was at the
time a suspect in another homicide. The date for the hit was
agreed as November 8, 2010. Jennifer had chosen it carefully,
knowing that her beloved brother, Felix, would not be at home.

Jennifer, however, was at home. And that was essential to the conspirator's plan. Shortly before retiring to bed that night, she snuck downstairs to unlock the front door. Then she went to her room and made a call, using a throw-away SIM card that had been given to her for that purpose. A short while later, Lenford Crawford, David Mylvaganam, and Eric Carty entered the Pan residence.

Hann and Bich Ha Pan were in their bedroom when three armed men suddenly burst in and started demanding money. The terrified couple was then forced down into the basement at gunpoint. There, Hann was pistol-whipped before the home invaders threw a blanket over his head. Moments later, five shots rang out. The killers then fled the scene, leaving the couple for dead.

It was a 911 call that brought the police to the Pan residence, a frantic, fearful call made by Jennifer Pan. The first responders found Jennifer shaken but unharmed. Her parents, though, had been gravely wounded. Bich had died where she'd been shot, while Hann had somehow managed to pull himself up the basement stairs, out of the house and onto the front lawn before collapsing. He was rushed to hospital, but the prognosis did not look good.

Detectives, meanwhile, had started questioning Jennifer. According to her, she'd been in her room when she'd heard a commotion from down the hall, her parents screaming and a voice she did not recognize shouting, "Where's the f**king money?"

Moments later, her bedroom door flew open and a masked man entered holding a gun. He demanded money, and Jennifer handed over $2,500 that she had saved up from her piano teaching job. The man then tied her hands behind her back and led her to her parents' bedroom, where Jennifer gave him a further $1,100 that she knew was hidden there. The man then tied her to a banister and ran downstairs. She heard several gunshots and then the sound of running, and then a car starting up outside. Eventually, she was able to free herself and that was when she called 911.

From the very start, the police felt that there was something not right with Jennifer Pan's story. For starters, this didn't look like your typical home invasion robbery. Very little had been taken. Hann's wallet, lying in plain sight, had been left untouched. So too was jewelry, expensive electronics and other valuables. Why go through the trouble of planning such an elaborate robbery and then leave behind most of the booty?

And there was no doubt at all that this had been planned. A security camera across the street from the Pan residence had captured footage of the gunmen pulling up in their car and then entering the house. There was no doubt at all that the Pans had been deliberately targeted. Why them? The police also could not understand why the elder Pans had been executed while Jennifer was left unharmed. If the intention of the robbers had been to eliminate witnesses, why leave one alive?

Those questions laid heavy on the detectives involved. But while they may have had their doubts about Jennifer's story, there was no evidence to suggest that she was anything but a victim of the tragedy. Despite police suspicion, it looked like Jennifer would not be charged. She would also be coming into a large inheritance.

Then a miracle happened. The bullet wound that Hann Pan had received to the head had rendered him comatose and, in the opinion of doctors, unlikely to recover. Yet, within days of the shooting, Hann was awake and ready to talk. What he had to say was shocking. He said that, as he and his wife were being dragged downstairs, he had seen his daughter engaged in hushed conversation with one of the home invaders. This, of course, contradicted everything that Jennifer had told the police. It moved her directly to the top of the suspect list.

Brought in for questioning, Jennifer initially feigned shock when she was asked about her involvement in the murder of her mother and the attempted murder of her father. But hours in a window-less interrogation room eventually wore her down. At times during the interrogation, she became so distraught that she curled up into a fetal position on the floor and refused to say anything. At other times, she sat hunched over, her face in her hands, weeping bitterly. It was only a matter of time before she cracked and the entire conspiracy was laid bare.

In short order, Daniel Wong, Lenford Crawford, David Mylvaganam, and Eric Carty were all in custody. Crawford, Mylvaganam, and Pan were tried together in March 2014, with each of them receiving a life sentence with no possibility of parole for at least 25 years. Carty was tried separately but received a similar sentence. Daniel Wong, who had played no part in the actual shooting, got a shorter term.

And so, Jennifer Pan was sent off to prison to complete a sentence that would see her behind bars at least into her fifties. Yet there are some who see her not as the villain of the piece but as a victim. These supporters claim that Jennifer was pushed to breaking point by her demanding and ambitious parents. There is validity to that argument, of course, but Jennifer was 24 years old at the time of the shooting and no longer under her parents' jurisdiction. She could just have walked away. Instead, she committed the ultimate betrayal.

For more True Crime books by Robert Keller

please visit:

http://bit.ly/kellerbooks